TAUGHT
AND
SCHOOLED BY
PAIN

Dr Herbert Mandla Mtowo

Taught and Schooled by Pain
Author: Dr Herbert Mandla Mtowo

Publisher: Editions Ratu Lali
Email: editions.ratulali@gmail.com
Chemin de Xhurdebise 6, 4960 Malmedy, Belgium

Mobile and Whatsapp: +32 470 688 302

ISBN: 978-2-931195-08-6
Deposit date: D/2024/15409/03
Our books are referred by Banque du Livre
in Belgium to the bookshops

CONTENTS

DEDICATION

To those who have walked through the fires of pain and emerged stronger. To all who have walked through the fires of adversity and emerged with newfound strength. To our beloved Gracious Mtowo, our beautiful daughter. You faced unimaginable loss at a tender age, losing your father (my brother), your mother, and your little sister all within a short time and you were only 5 years. Yet, despite such heartache, you have risen with strength and resilience. Today, your star shines brightly as you embrace life to the fullest in the UAE. I love you kiddo and marvel at God given strengths that has seen you through.

We are so proud of the incredible woman you've become, living a life that honours' the memories of those we've lost. To my dear big sister, Sisi Sophia—a true model and source of inspiration to me, the steadfast pillar of the Mtowo siblings. You have been nothing short of incredible. When Bra Gersham passed on, you stepped up without hesitation, caring for his children, Betty and Basil. And again, when Bra Robson and his wife passed, you embraced their nine-month-old baby and Gracious with open arms and a loving heart. I am constantly in awe of the God-given strength and resilience that you are blessed with and, guiding you through these selfless acts. You are truly a gift to our family.

This book is dedicated to the ones who have faced life's greatest challenges and chose to see them as teachers.

To those who have lost, yet found purpose; who have hurt, yet discovered compassion; who have fallen, yet risen stronger. To the resilient souls who understand that pain, though uninvited, can be a profound source of wisdom. This book is dedicated to those who, despite beginning life under the weight of adversity, dared to dream and transform their lives. It is for those raised in broken homes or difficult environments, who grew up feeling abandoned or unworthy, yet chose not to be defined by these circumstances. To those told they were destined for failure, who faced labels of inadequacy, yet pushed past every doubt to build a future of purpose and achievement.

This dedication goes out to those whose experiences in love left them feeling rejected or labelled as unworthy of companionship, but who discovered a love that embraced and cherished them completely. It celebrates those who faced educational setbacks, forced to leave school not by choice but by circumstance, who later climbed the ladder of success through sheer grit and determination. This book is for those who defied society's odds and built legacies that shine through their achievements in academics, careers, families, and relationships.

May this book serve as a testament to your resilience and a reminder that from the depths of struggle can arise stories of triumph, grace, and enduring love. May you find comfort in knowing you are not alone and may your courage to learn from pain continue to inspire others.

This is for you—who were taught and schooled by life's hardest lessons and grew not in spite of them but because of them.

This book is for you, the resilient souls who find wisdom through hardship.

'Pain insists upon being attended to. God whispers to us in our pleasures, speaks in our consciences, but shouts in our pains: it is His megaphone to rouse a deaf world.'
C.S. Lewis

'In the heart of adversity, there emerges a beauty that defies its surroundings—a brilliantly coloured flower thriving in a barren landscape.' This flower stands resilient and vivid against all odds, a symbol of hope and tenacity. In the same way, pain and struggle often shape us into something unexpectedly beautiful, fostering strength where there was once only hardship.

Being taught and schooled by pain is like this flower's journey; it may feel as though life's challenges have left us in a desolate place. Yet, the very barrenness of our surroundings allows our resilience and inner beauty to emerge more vividly. The adversity becomes a backdrop that highlights the strength, courage, and grace that pain has cultivated in us.

Like the flower, our growth in times of hardship reflects the quiet beauty of endurance.

It shows us that even in the most desolate landscapes of life, we are capable of blossoming—radiant and resilient—proving that hardship does not strip away our potential but rather sets the stage for its most profound display.

This journey through pain transforms us into a testament of survival and a beacon of hope, as we continue to thrive against all odds.'

Dr Herbert Mandla Mtowo

FOREWORD

Pain is a word most of us instinctively recoil from. It is an experience we seek to avoid, an unwelcome companion in life's journey. Yet, as much as we try to escape it, pain remains a constant. It appears in countless forms, from the physical pangs of injury to the emotional ache of heartbreak, from the grief of loss to the gnawing despair of personal failure. This book, Taught and Schooled by Pain, is a testament to the idea that pain, as difficult and often relentless as it may be, can be one of life's most profound teachers.

In these pages, you will find not only stories of hardship but also revelations of transformation. What sets this book apart is its compassionate, honest approach to understanding pain as something beyond suffering. It suggests that rather than merely enduring our challenges, we can allow pain to teach us, shape us, and guide us toward the life we are meant to lead. In this way, Taught and Schooled by Pain is both a guide and a conversation with the reader, inviting them to view pain through a different lens—not as a punishment, but as a pathway. This book is birthed out of my life's painful experiences, from losing my dear mother Betty who was a pillar of strength in my life and our family, to my losing my example of a warrior and strong man, my dad, even to arrive at his funeral when he was already laid to rest.

The anguish and pain of losing my four brothers and little sister Joylene was so devastating and three of my brother's funerals and burials I missed them.

Pain has shaped my behaviours and personalities and given me a new perspective to life and the future. talk of physical pain, emotional pain I have walked that journey and it hasn't been easy, this book is meant to inspire millions to be champions, rise from the dust of life`s ashes. My life is a like a never-ending book you would want to read forever, at being told its over (relationship break-up) at the police station, being locked at police cells for a couple weeks, and at being admitted in hospital and bedridden for months and being pushed on wheelchair and you name them all. And not so long ago in Zambia 2022, as one of the passengers in a bus that caught fire, and people screaming for life and jumping through the windows and pushing and shoving the door, I have a deep cut on my stomach from the terrifying ordeal where other heads were split and into two other died. Life has been really kind and gracious to me.

What has been crystal clear to me over the years is that pain can't be ignored it demands our attention, pulling us away from distractions and requiring us to focus on the very essence of what it means to be human. In confronting pain, we often confront ourselves, discovering aspects of our character that would remain hidden in moments of ease and comfort. Pain pushes us to redefine our resilience, expand our empathy, and test the strength of our values and convictions. Pain doesn't merely happen to us; it transforms us, if we allow it. I have lost many battles in life; I have lost countless times but despite all these difficult circumstances I have incredibly grown.

This book offers you the insight into this transformation journey myself and many others have walked through. Each chapter examines a unique dimension of pain, from loss and heartbreak to resilience and renewal, providing

not only narratives but practical reflections. It encourages readers to sit with their pain, to consider what it has to teach, and to emerge not unscathed but refined.

As you begin this journey through the pages of Taught and Schooled by Pain, be prepared to see aspects of yourself reflected in the stories and insights I share about in this book. Let this book be a companion as you explore what it means to grow through your struggles. Remember, you are not alone in this journey; countless others have found themselves in the classroom of pain, emerging wiser, more compassionate, and more resilient.

In life this dawned on me and helped me grow that, we may not choose pain, but we can choose what it will mean to us. It is my hope that this book provides you with a map, a mirror, and a measure of courage as you allow pain to teach you, shape you, and ultimately, to lead you to a richer, deeper understanding of life.

Dr Herbert Mandla Mtowo

WORD OF ASSISTANT PROFESSOR MUNYA MUJURU-(USA-TEXAS)

In a world that often seeks to avoid discomfort, pain is a subject we frequently shy away from. Yet, it is an undeniable part of the human experience—a teacher that comes uninvited yet holds invaluable lessons within its depths. In Taught and Schooled by Pain, Dr. Herbert Mandla Mtowo invites us to confront the complexities of pain with courage and compassion.

Dr. Mtowo's exploration is not merely an academic examination of suffering; it is a heartfelt journey that resonates with his lived experiences and of many. Through personal anecdotes, insights from clinical practice, and stories of those who have navigated their own struggles, this book illuminates the transformative potential of pain. It encourages us to recognize that every hardship we endure can become a stepping stone toward growth, resilience, and a deeper understanding of ourselves.

As a respected figure in the mental health community, Dr. Mtowo has dedicated his life to helping others find meaning in their struggles. His compassionate approach underscores the importance of vulnerability and connection in the healing process. He shows us that by embracing our pain, we open the door to profound personal transformation and greater empathy for the experiences of others.

This book serves as a guide for anyone grappling with their own pain, as well as those who wish to support others on their journeys. It is an invitation to explore the intricate relationship between suffering and healing, urging readers to view their challenges not as obstacles but as essential components of their personal narratives.

In the pages that follow, you will find a roadmap to resilience—a path that encourages reflection, fosters understanding, and ultimately empowers you to rise from your struggles stronger and more aligned with your true self. Dr. Mtowo reminds us that we are not defined by our pain, but by how we choose to grow through it.

I invite you to embark on this transformative journey. Embrace the lessons that pain has to offer and allow them to guide you toward a deeper sense of purpose and connection. This book is a testament to the resilience of the human spirit and the profound growth that can arise from even the darkest moments.

Assistant Professor Munya Mujuru-(USA-Texas)

INTRODUCTION

Rewriting Taught and Schooled by Pain five years later, from the time I first wrote this book emerged from a pivotal pause in my life, following a series of harrowing experiences. It began with painful moments during my time bedridden at Steve Biko Hospital (2021), where I spent three months in the ICU. After being discharged, I was attacked on the streets of Pretoria's CBD, resulting in three broken ribs. This led to another hospitalization, and soon I found myself on a wheelchair in Walvis Bay, Namibia. (2022)

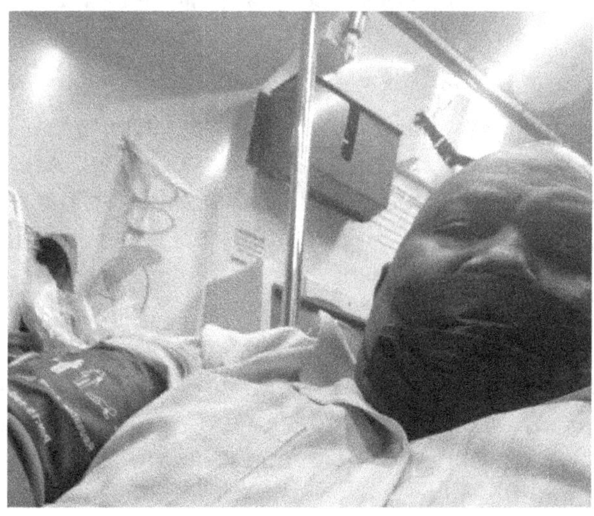

As if that wasn't enough, I was later involved in a catastrophic bus accident in Zambia (2022), where the bus caught fire and was reduced to ashes. I sustained a deep cut on my abdomen, and tragically, others lost their lives in the incident. Looking back today, I still feel numb, constantly questioning, *'Did I really make it out of all that?'*

Taught and Schooled by Pain shares my real-life stories alongside those of many others who have faced adversity and emerged victorious. It is a testament to the resilience of the human spirit, highlighting how we can all become champions in life despite the challenges we endure.

Pain, in all its forms, is perhaps one of life's most universal experiences. No matter who we are or where we come from, at some point, we will encounter it—sometimes briefly, like a fleeting disappointment, and other times with an intensity that redefines our lives.

This book, Taught and Schooled by Pain, explores the paradox of pain as both an unwanted affliction and an invaluable teacher, guiding us toward resilience, self-awareness, and empathy. Fasten your sit belts as I take you on this ride and life`s mysterious journey of pain.

Our instinct is often to avoid pain, to minimize its impact, or to anesthetize it in whatever way possible. But what if pain, rather than merely being something to escape, could be a path toward personal transformation? What if the wounds we incur—whether physical, emotional, or existential—are gateways to deeper understanding, fostering resilience and helping us grow into the truest versions of ourselves? I ask again sobering question, 'What if' Remember Joseph in the bible. His pain was the path and guide to sustaining his brothers and family and so the nation of Israel. I ask again what if we knew it would pan out beautifully like this.

This book is an invitation to shift our perspective on pain, seeing it not solely as a cause of suffering but as a form of education. While pain can feel isolated, it also has a remarkable power to connect us. By reflecting on our own experiences of hardship, we often find common ground with others who have faced similar challenges.

Pain, in its many forms, is a profound leveler; it reminds us that despite our differences, we share in the same human vulnerabilities.

In different chapters in this book, I address a different aspect of how pain shapes us.

I will delve into pain's role as a teacher, exploring how it can deepen our empathy, build our resilience, and even clarify our purpose. From loss and failure to heartbreak and healing, each experience of pain is examined through a lens of growth, allowing us to see our most difficult moments as part of a larger narrative.

In one of the chapters, I explore with you how enduring hardship develops our inner strength, often revealing facets of ourselves we might otherwise overlook. Even Apostle Paul of the bible, says, *'Our suffering is not in vain, there is a glory that awaits us'*, we'll confront the concept of resilience, asking what it means to bounce back from adversity and how each painful experience leaves us more grounded and capable of facing life's uncertainties. In one chapter, *'Pain's Lesson Hidden in Suffering'*, take you through into the transformative nature of grief, discovering how it often reshapes our priorities and clarifies what truly matters.

Throughout the book, you will find stories and insights from individuals who have faced pain in ways both universal and unique. Their experiences serve as reminders that while pain is a solitary experience, it also connects us to a shared human story.

You'll read of those who have found ways to not only survive their suffering but to embrace it as a source of strength and wisdom.

In a world that values comfort and efficiency, the idea of learning from pain can feel counterintuitive.

Yet history, literature, and philosophy are full of figures who found purpose and insight through hardship. From the stoics who emphasized resilience to modern-day thinkers who view suffering as a source of strength, there is an undeniable power in the idea of pain as an education. This book builds on that perspective, arguing that our most painful moments, though challenging, are often the very experiences that teach us compassion, courage, and authenticity.

Taught and Schooled by Pain is not simply a book about pain—it is a book about life. It has taken me more than ten years to write this book, and the chapter was birthed out of my own painful life`s experiences. It is an invitation to reflect on your own experiences, to find meaning in hardship, and to allow pain to transform you in ways that foster growth, connection, and purpose. Whether you are navigating a painful chapter of your life right now or looking back on past challenges, may this book be a companion and a guide, illuminating the possibility of growth through every trial.

In reading these pages, you will discover that while pain is inevitable, it does not have to be in vain. It can shape us, refine us, and ultimately, lead us to a life of greater depth and understanding.

Pain, when embraced as a teacher, becomes not only something we endure but something that fundamentally enriches our lives. Job says. *'Though He slay me, yet will I glory in Him'*.

SPECIAL THANKS TO

Ma Tirzha, *(Ms Tirzha Stutzer)*

From the first time we met at a conference in Windhoek, I felt an instant connection with you. You embraced me with such warmth and understanding, and I knew from that moment that I had found someone truly special. You became a pillar of strength during the hardest times of my life, especially when I lost my three brothers while I was already blessed to be your mentee. You loved me like a mother, and being welcomed into your life was the beginning of my healing and recovery. You gave me a second chance—a chance to live fully again. Your love knows no boundaries, extending not only to me but also to so many others.

I am deeply honored to call you, my Ma. The story of my life would be incomplete without you; you are woven into every chapter, shaping who I am today. My world opened up simply because of your love and your unwavering belief in growth and fruitfulness. For over fifteen years now, you have been a mother, mentor, leader, and guiding light in my life.

Twice, I have faced death: first with an illness that still feels unfathomable, and later after a horrific bus accident in Zambia. In both moments, you stood by me with a love that rekindled my hope and gave me a reason to smile again. Your selfless nature, nurturing spirit, and ability to see potential in everyone you meet, despite their background or struggles, is nothing short of inspiring. You always said that seeing growth and fruitfulness brings you happiness—and it's clear you have dedicated your life to fostering that in others.

I remember a specific day when I was gravely ill, and you took me to the hospital. In that moment, someone looked at you and said, *'Ma, can you just let Herbert go and die among his sisters?'* I'll never forget how you responded— your voice soft yet firm as you replied that such a decision was not for them to make. That moment showed me the depth of your love, your boundless compassion, and your fierce commitment to my well-being.

Through everything, you've given me not only a home but a space where I can grow and be myself under your guidance. For that, I am eternally grateful. You have shown me love beyond measure, and I pray that God continues to use you to touch and transform lives, bringing hope to those who need it most.

You gave me a roof over my head during one of the most difficult times of my life, after I was arrested and locked up over an unfounded scandal. It was my first time experiencing the darkness of a police cell, and I was thousands of kilometres' away from family. You took me in with open arms, providing me not only with shelter but also a safe place to process everything.

In your motherly way, you knew I needed time and space. You never pressured me to explain; instead, you allowed me to be in solitude, respecting the silence I needed to heal. Occasionally, you would simply say, *'Sometimes it's good to gather and pray with others.'* Those words, gentle yet encouraging, were exactly what I needed.

To Ma Tirzah, I want to express my heartfelt gratitude for your unwavering support of my dream and vision to cultivate entrepreneurship in Africa.

Your encouragement and belief in my mission have been nothing short of humbling, especially during the launch of this initiative of Africa Entrepreneurs Networks.

It is incredibly significant to me that this launch took place in your space, and I am truly honored that you provided me with a property and office to grow my business and operate from. Your generosity has given me the foundation I needed to pursue my goals and has instilled in me a sense of confidence that I will carry forward.

I am still speechless at the extent of your support, and I deeply appreciate the trust you have placed in me. Your commitment to nurturing aspiring entrepreneurs will undoubtedly have a lasting impact on many lives, and I am grateful to be part of this journey with you. Thank you for believing in me and for being a guiding light as I work to make this vision a reality.

From the bottom of my heart, I am endlessly grateful to you and God.

Thank you, Ma.

To my Mum and Dad,

I am deeply grateful to you for the gift of life and for instilling in me the invaluable principles of strength and hard work. These guiding values have shaped my journey and remain at the core of who I am. It saddens me that you couldn't stay longer to witness the person I am becoming today. Deep down, I know, Mum, that you would be proud of me—I miss you dearly. Though it's been many years since you left, it feels as though it was just yesterday.

With love and gratitude,

Dear God,

Thank you for the gift of life and salvation. I am deeply grateful for Your presence in my life and for the many teachings that have guided me, shared by pastors who have invested in my spiritual journey. Your grace has been my strength, and Your wisdom my light.

With gratitude and reverence

Dear Helena Bossers,

Helena, words cannot fully express my gratitude for having you as my nurse, sister, and family. I remember how, during some of my lowest moments, you were there, providing care with such warmth and encouragement. Your compassion and commitment to my well-being lifted my spirits more than you could know. The bond I share with you and Pieter has become one of my life's greatest blessings. From checking in on my health to offering help during busy times, your support has been unwavering.
When I was involved in the bus accident in Zambia, you and Ma showered me with care, even going so far as to replace my broken laptop—a gesture I never expected.

Helena, thank you for your boundless love and support.

To Bekezela,

Thank you for the precious gifts of lovely children, Roberta and Jordan. I am forever grateful to you for bringing these two incredible lives into the world. Your dedication and love as their mother have been truly remarkable, and I pray that God rewards you abundantly for all you have done and continue to do for them. The memories I share with them are priceless and will forever be cherished.

With deep gratitude.

To my beloved sisi, Mrs Sophia Musariri (nee Mtowo),

Thank you for being a constant pillar of strength in my life. You have always been there, stepping up with grace and resilience when our family needed you most. Your unwavering love and selflessness, especially when you took in Betty, Basil, and Gracious after our brothers' passing, have shown me the true meaning of family.

I am endlessly inspired by your heart and commitment, and I am so grateful to have you as my big sister. Your courage and support have been a blessing to us all. Family matters so deep to you and you always encourage me to plan and grow family and business.

With all my love and respect.

To biggie Alpheus Shindi,

You are, and will always be, my big brother. You've given me the gift of experiencing the pride and comfort of having an older brother, especially when all my other brothers were taken too soon from my life. Through it all, you made time for me, you showed me love, and you never hesitated to offer guidance and correction. You held my hand and led me toward greatness, always reminding me of my purpose.

Your words echo in my heart: *'Younger, God's hand is over your life. He wants to use you for His greatness.'*

These words have been my anchor and my reminder, helping me to rise above challenges and stay focused on the path I am meant to walk.

Big Brother, you have stood by me through my lowest moments, through difficult health challenges, and through painful relationship struggles. You've been my steadfast support, my buckler, and my voice of reason, offering strength when I needed it most.

For your unwavering presence and wisdom, I am deeply grateful. Thank you for being a guiding light in my life.

For your love, wisdom, and belief in me,

I am forever grateful.

Professor Mahlangu and Mama Dee,

To Professor Mahlangu and Mama Dee, thank you for the incredible impact you've had on my life. Professor Mahlangu, your mentorship and wisdom have guided me through pivotal moments, helping me shape my purpose and deepen my knowledge. Your dedication to my growth has been both inspiring and humbling.

Mama Dee, your warmth and unwavering support have been a source of comfort and strength. You've given me a sense of belonging, treating me with kindness and encouragement during times of uncertainty.

Both of you have been instrumental in my journey, and I am profoundly grateful for the ways you've helped me move forward, even in my most challenging times.

Thank you for being pillars in my life and for your ongoing belief in me.

A Tribute to Myself & Many Others,

I want to take a moment to express my gratitude to myself and to the many academicians, helping hands, destiny helpers, and even strangers who, at various points, embraced me, gave me hope, and helped me see beyond pain and trials. To myself—Herbert—thank you for not giving up, even when there were countless reasons to do so.

In times when abandoning the many God-driven, life-affirming, and community-focused initiatives you hold dear would have been the easier path, you chose instead to persevere.

Despite feeling overwhelmed and facing setbacks from all directions, you found the strength to rise time and again. Life has certainly not been a bed of roses; rather, it has been filled with thorns, losses, rejections, and heartbreaks. Yet, here you are, standing strong and resolute, declaring, *'The sun will rise again, and we will try once more.'* This journey, though fraught with challenges, has been worth every step. You've demonstrated resilience in the face of adversity, and your determination continues to inspire not only others but also yourself. Thank you for holding on and believing in the promise of tomorrow. Thank you all, from the depths of my heart. Your support, kindness, and encouragement have been an anchor and a light in my journey.

With all my love and gratitude.

getting it REAL
with DR PRINCE HERBERT
"The more you talk about it ,
The more free you will feel"

ACKNOWLEDGMENTS

The journey of writing Taught and Schooled by Pain has been a profound experience, made possible by the contributions and support of many individuals who have guided me along the way, my own life`s experiences have shaped and inspired me to write this book. I will be doing workshops trainings and speaking platforms based on this book and chapters in this book.

I would like to express my deepest gratitude to my family and friends, whose unwavering love and encouragement have been a source of strength throughout this endeavour. Your belief in me has inspired me to persevere even during the most challenging moments of this writing process.

I am especially thankful to my mentors and colleagues in, psychology and mental health field, whose insights and expertise have enriched my understanding of pain and resilience. Your willingness to share your knowledge and experiences has profoundly influenced my work and the practical ideas presented in this book. Thank you for your guidance and for being beacons of wisdom.

To the individuals who shared their stories with me and allowed me to include your life`s stories in this book, I am grateful and appreciate you deeply, your courage to confront your pain and articulate your journeys has provided invaluable perspectives.

Your experiences remind us that we are not alone in our struggles and that healing is possible.

I am honored to have been entrusted with your narratives and to weave them into this work.

I would also like to acknowledge the researchers and authors whose works have informed and inspired my writing. The literature on trauma, healing, and resilience has been an essential foundation for this book. Your contributions to the field continue to illuminate the complexities of the human experience.

Lastly, I extend my heartfelt thanks to my readers. It is my hope that this book serves as a source of encouragement and inspiration as you navigate your own journeys through pain. Your willingness to engage with these themes and seek growth in your struggles is a testament to the resilience of the human spirit.

Together, we embark on a transformative journey toward healing, resilience, and personal growth. Thank you for being a part of this exploration.

1.
UNDERSTANDING PAIN AS A TEACHER

'Pain is the best teacher, but no one wants
to go to its class.'
Unknown

In this book and mostly this opening chapter. I share with you some of my most painful life`s experiences which have become my best lectures on life`s issues. By understanding pain as a teacher, I explore with you the profound role that pain has played and will play in shaping our lives, beliefs, and personal growth. Far from being a mere adversary, pain can serve as a guide, signaling where change, growth, or acceptance is needed, it all depends how you take your painful difficult moments in life as punishment or learning curve. In this chapter I delve into the nature of pain as a necessary aspect of the human experience, its transformative potential, and the wisdom it can impart. Throughout my own life`s stories and others, who have allowed me to share with you the reader their life's stories, psychological insights, and reflections, you will be encouraged to reframe your relationship with pain and see it not as a foe but as a valuable teacher that deepens resilience, empathy, and self-awareness.

In our culture, pain is often viewed as something to be avoided, masked, or hurried through—a disruption in our journey rather than a necessary part of it.

But from my own life's experiences, I have found that pain, whether physical, emotional, or spiritual, is an inevitable force, woven into the fabric of human experience. Pain is not merely a disruption; it has been to me and is a profound teacher that brings us face-to-face with the deepest parts of ourselves, urging us toward growth, resilience, and compassion. The bible in the book of John reiterates and says, *'Unless a grain of wheat falls into the ground and dies, it shall abide alone.'* There is seed bearing and life in the dying to self and the process of becoming in life. The inevitability of pain is one of life's most unyielding truths. From the pain of childhood scrapes and bruises to the complex emotional pains of adulthood—loss, heartbreak, illness, grief—we are consistently reminded that pain is inescapable. This inevitability may feel daunting, yet it is pain's very constancy that teaches us some of life's most essential lessons.

Throughout history and literature, pain has been metaphorically described as a teacher or a guide. Philosophers, poets, and thinkers have long argued that pain, though difficult, is an instrument of self-discovery and wisdom. Fyodor Dostoevsky wrote, *'Pain and suffering are always inevitable for a large intelligence and a deep heart.'*

His words suggest that those who live fully and deeply must also be open to pain as part of their understanding. To embrace life fully is to be open to its highs and lows, its joys and inevitable sorrows.

Pain does not merely create suffering; it reshapes us, often revealing facets of ourselves we may never have known otherwise. When we face loss or heartbreak, we learn about our capacity to endure.

Through injury, we learn the delicate balance of the human body and the fragility of life. Pain, then, not only tests our limits but also expands them, illuminating our potential for resilience.

When pain is viewed as an enemy, our instinct is to run from it or numb it. However, when we accept pain as a natural part of our journey, we allow ourselves to learn from it. In her work on loss and healing, author Elisabeth Kübler-Ross said, *'The reality is that you will grieve forever. You will not 'get over' the loss of a loved one; you will learn to live with it.'* Kübler-Ross's insight reveals an essential truth about growth: some pains do not disappear but become integrated into our lives. By learning to live with pain, we develop resilience, patience, and understanding.

Just as muscles grow stronger through the resistance of weights, emotional and spiritual growth often comes from bearing the weight of life's hardships. We learn patience through frustration, empathy through loss, courage through fear. Pain, then, is not a mere affliction but a gateway to personal transformation.

Is it not only remarkable and divine that you easily connect with people who have either gone and overcame same life's challenges as you have done without you asking them but by mere connecting? Pain has such a remarkable ability to foster connections. Those who have endured similar challenges often find solace in one another, bonding over shared struggles.

Not as victims but sharing stories of victory and triumph, by writing this book my focus is not on the victim, or trying to form a victim's club, but putting it in black and write how winners and champions have been shaped through pain. Life is full of stories of mighty men and women who fell and rose up and again to defy odds. The Bible is also very clear that it's not in the falling but in the rising, when it says, *'The righteous falls seven times but the Lord raises them again'*. And as novelist Haruki Murakami put it, *'Pain is inevitable. Suffering is optional.'* This insight speaks to the role of shared suffering in building compassion; while we may all experience pain differently, the universality of it connects us to each other. Welcome to my book, where I teach you that we all get bogged down and fall, but we have to rise up and stand strong again.

In times of shared pain—whether as individuals or societies—we experience a rare clarity of purpose. In these moments, we realize we are part of something larger/bigger, reminding us that while pain is an individual experience, it is also one of humanity's most universal experiences. The bible even goes on to say, *'They overcame the devil by words of their testimonies'*. There is strength and power in shared stories of one's pain that turned victorious chapters in one's life.

Accepting the inevitability of pain allows us to approach life's hardships with a different mindset. Rather than viewing pain as an interruption, we can see it as an essential part of our story. We cannot always choose our suffering, but we can choose our response to it.

Instead of allowing pain to close us off, we can allow it to open us to new insights, connections, and strengths.

The inevitability of pain, when accepted, becomes a path not just of survival but of transformation. It may take time, courage, and patience, but by embracing pain rather than denying it, we gain wisdom, compassion, and ultimately, a deeper understanding of what it means to be human. Pain, as inevitable as it may be, is a profound reminder that we are alive, resilient, and capable of immense growth.

Along the journey of life, I had to accept reality that pain is part of the package and until we accept pain as part of life, many of us will forever struggle in life over things that we have no control of, pain is not for the poor only, or uneducated but all mankind, rich or poor, believers or not, not educated or not, all mankind will face pain. The bible is even clear through the words of Job, *'Man that is born of a woman of a of a few days but full of trouble'*

So, by understanding that pain, whether physical, emotional, or existential, is a universal experience. Pain, in many forms, shapes all of us, regardless of background or life circumstances.

There bare types of Pain that we all go through I will just go through them quickly for our understanding and growths and helping others. Differentiating between acute and chronic pain, physical versus emotional pain, and understanding how each type can serve as a unique teacher.

When we have that new perspective of suffering, we have passed the first step to embracing pain and realising it is part of our teaching classrooms requirements in life. Life`s Challenging the instinct to resist or avoid pain entirely and opening the mind to see it as an integral part of growth and understanding.

Let me remind you that life is a self-discovery through our both good and painful experiences that we go through and shape us, our personalities and characters. Pain reveals the depths of our unknown or unrevealed parts of our being we learn to prioritize in life based on painful experiences we go through. Exploring how pain can reveal what truly matters to us, highlighting our deepest fears, vulnerabilities, and core values.

In my own personal life`s experiences, I realized that lessons of resilience were shaped in the furnace of fiery painful life`s journey.

It is beyond doubt that pain makes it clear, how enduring and confronting pain can cultivate strength and a capacity to withstand life's hardships.

I learnt to realize hidden emotions through life`s painful doses. One will come to a point of realization that unresolved pain often masks hidden emotions like fear, grief, or anger, which, when acknowledged, can lead to healing and clarity. Unacknowledged emotional pain can be both destructive and toxic to an individual. When pain is suppressed or ignored, it doesn't simply vanish; rather, it festers beneath the surface, affecting mental, emotional, and even physical well-being. Left unchecked, this unaddressed pain can manifest as anxiety, depression, or anger, sometimes leading to destructive behaviours and strained relationships.

Carrying unacknowledged emotional pain often acts like a hidden toxin, eroding self-worth and hindering personal growth. It can cloud judgment, disrupt focus, and impact one's ability to connect authentically with others. Over time, the weight of unaddressed pain can lead to a sense of isolation, as the individual may feel misunderstood or disconnected from those around them.

Acknowledging and processing pain, on the other hand, is a step toward healing and freedom. It allows individuals to confront their experiences, understand their feelings, and regain control over their lives. By bringing pain into the light, one can begin to heal, build resilience, and ultimately transform hardship into a source of strength and empathy.

Take not that pain is most powerful force of transformation, pain transforms us.

Since time immemorial and bible times pain has always ben and still remains a catalyst for growth that is why you and me will realise how significant challenges and painful experiences often serve as turning points, leading to personal growth, maturity, and self-improvement.

Being empathetic is not an easy expression, but many countless times we learn how to be empathetic through our own suffering experiences. To recognize how personal suffering enables us to relate to others' pain, deepening our compassion, patience, and understanding toward others, is growth and learning place.

We develop a growth mindset mostly when we are put in difficult places or situations. Encouraging a shift from viewing pain as punishment to seeing it as a challenge that reveals new strengths and insights.

Growth and peace happen when we begin to look at pain as an ally and not an adversary. You and me and many others need to embrace pain as a teacher fi we are to have peace and serenity in the journey of life. Learning to view pain not with resentment but as a mentor that highlights our needs, limits, and personal path to healing.

Most people who are grumpy, angry, stressed, frustrated are so because they keep fighting pain in whatever form it is, especially being unjustly treated, lied at, you name them all painful life`s situations.

By so doing resisting or denying pain often amplifies suffering, whereas acceptance can bring clarity, peace, and direction.

Pain plays a huge role in forging ahead with life`s purpose and meaning. It sounds absurd to say, but truth be told there is purpose in pain. Life`s experiences of pain can give rise to new purposes, such as advocacy, personal projects, or creative pursuits that bring meaning and fulfillment.

Find in your space examples of men and women who have built their life`s purposes from pain. Real-life stories of people who transformed painful experiences into positive contributions, helping others and building legacies rooted in resilience.

Let pain usher you into growth and growth mindset mode. The idea of 'post-traumatic growth'—how hardships can, in the long term, contribute to a stronger, more insightful version of oneself. I have done and accomplished more and a lot after most of my painful experiences in life`s darkest moments.

Below are some, great techniques which you can practically apply to learn from pain.

Learn to do reflective practices such as; Journaling prompts and mindfulness exercises to reflect on personal pain and extract its teachings.

Always learn to build supportive systems which is for your good. The role of trusted friends, counsellors, or spiritual guides in helping us navigate and process painful experiences.

Grow the habit of journaling and create pain wisdom journal, journaling. A guided exercise to document moments of growth, realizations, and strengths gained through pain, fostering a constructive perspective on past challenges.

Let healing flow and allow the process to go uninterrupted it's for your good. Such techniques like therapy, community support, physical care, or spiritual practices help us manage pain constructively.

You will go through incredible growth while you are healing. By all means balance the acceptance of pain's lessons with the active pursuit of healing, cultivating resilience while finding pathways to relief and peace.

Here are some important take aways from this chapter you can glean and learn from.

a. Remember pain as a teacher and not your enemy. By reframing pain as a guide, we can embrace its role in our growth and learn from the insights it offers.
b. By you extracting meaning from suffering you will not only grow but find meaning and peace.
c. Pain often reveals our values, strengths, and purpose, helping us live more intentionally and with a greater sense of empathy.
d. We must all transform our pain into purpose. Rather than allowing pain to define or diminish us, we can use it as fuel to grow, heal, and contribute positively ereto our own lives and others.

In this chapter I invite you to take a step back from your pain and see it through a new lens, offering tools for reflection, self-compassion, and resilience-building. By understanding pain as a teacher, you and I learn to harness its transformative power and find meaning and purpose even amidst life's hardships.

2.
THE ROOTS OF PAIN
(Physical, emotional, and spiritual)

'Growth begins where comfort ends.'
Unknown

In The Roots of Pain – Physical, Emotional, and Spiritual, we examine the multifaceted nature of pain, recognizing that it goes beyond the physical to include emotional and spiritual dimensions. In this chapter I delve into the different types of pain we encounter throughout life, exploring how each affects us uniquely and can shape our behavior, beliefs, and relationships. By understanding the origins and impacts of these varied forms of pain, you and me will gain insight into the complexities of the human experience and the role each type plays in personal growth, healing, and resilience.

We should look at pain also beyond the physical discomfort. Defining pain in its various forms—physical, emotional, and spiritual—and how each impacts our overall well-being. Pain comes and rearranges our entire lives, mindsets, thinking process and way of doing things it can either be negatively of positively.

Pain is so interconnected by its nature that one segment of life's pain affects all areas of one's life. How physical, emotional, and spiritual pain often overlap, affecting one another and creating a cumulative impact.

Pain is often seen as an isolating experience, a solitary trial that disconnects us from others as we navigate personal hardship. Yet, paradoxically, pain has an immense power to unite, creating connections that may otherwise remain dormant. Pain transcends cultural, social, and generational boundaries, reminding us that, despite our differences, we share in this profoundly human experience. It can foster empathy, deepen relationships, and encourage a sense of community as we come to understand that we are all part of a collective journey marked by both joy and suffering. During the process of writing this second edition of this book, I as an InterNations Global Consul, I had the privileged to host an event with an audience of 200+ participants' from over 100 countries emotional healing. What was clear during this event was the connectedness of people through pain as a global community, shared stories pain and triumphantly overcoming, made it clear that pain is universal language that easily connects people despite colours and cultural differences.

Along the journey of life, you will realise that pain is the bridge to empathy. At its core, the interconnectedness of pain is rooted in empathy. When we experience pain— whether through personal loss, failure, or hardship—we gain insight into the struggles of others. We come to understand the weight of grief, the sting of rejection, or the ache of loneliness, and this understanding opens our hearts to others going through similar challenges. In this way, pain becomes a bridge, linking us to a broader, shared human experience.

Philosopher Simone Weil captured this idea, saying, *'The love of our neighbour in all its fullness simply means being able to say, 'What are you going through?'*

Empathy arising from pain is not merely theoretical; it is deeply felt and transformative. When we see our own experiences reflected in others, we gain an intimate understanding of their emotions, often creating bonds of compassion and support. These connections, born of shared struggles, cultivate a profound sense of belonging that only grows stronger as we lean on one another.

The joy of pain at communal levels is that it brings healing and fosters community strengths and community resilience. Beyond individual empathy, pain has the potential to unite communities. These collective traumas—such as natural disasters, public crises, or shared losses—draws people together, often breaking down social barriers that would otherwise keep them apart. But history has a record of communities experiencing collective pain and known to coming together to support each other, offering practical assistance and emotional solidarity. This shared suffering becomes a unifying force, fostering a sense of resilience that extends beyond individuals to entire groups. We see this in disaster response efforts, in memorials honouring collective loss, and in the solidarity of movements aimed at justice and healing.

In the midst of collective pain, there is often a renewed sense of purpose and unity. People rally around shared causes, finding common ground in their experiences.

This sense of interconnectedness reminds us that our pain is not something we bear alone but a part of a larger tapestry of human experience.

Many a times if not mostly the journey of self-discovery and growth is spurred or triggered by life`s painful moments. We take stork and introspectively into ourselves when we have had a close shave with painful experiences. Pain also connects us internally to our own selves, illuminating parts of our character that might otherwise remain hidden. When we experience pain, we are often stripped of our usual defences, forced to confront aspects of ourselves that we may not fully understand. This introspection can lead to personal transformation, helping us become more self-aware, resilient, and compassionate individuals. In a way, pain connects us to our deepest truths, clarifying what we value and what we are capable of enduring.

As we grow through our own pain, we become more attuned to the experiences of others. We understand the universality of suffering and learn to approach others with an open heart, knowing that each person carries their own struggles. This deepened self-understanding brings us closer to others, reinforcing the interconnectedness of our journeys.

We are wired differently in life, and our personalities reflect our differences in our cultures', way of life and colour differences' but this one thing I know. Pain makes us one people and one blood.

But despite all these our many differences, pain is a language that everyone understands. Whether we come from different cultures, backgrounds, or belief systems, pain is an experience that crosses all boundaries. It is a constant in human life, transcending the specific details of our individual stories. We may not share the same experiences, but we share in the understanding of struggle, and this creates a language of compassion that binds us together.

In this way, pain reminds us that we are not isolated beings; we are part of a larger, interconnected web of humanity. Our struggles, while deeply personal, contribute to a collective story. And as we learn from one another's experiences, we find strength, hope, and healing in the knowledge that we are not alone.

By understanding the interconnectedness of pain is ultimately an invitation to embrace our shared humanity. By acknowledging that pain is something we all experience, we can move toward a world that values compassion, empathy, and mutual support. Pain does not have to isolate us; instead, it can bring us together, teaching us that we are more alike than we are different. As we learn to carry each other's burdens, we find that pain, far from being a solely negative experience, can become a powerful force for connection, unity, and healing.

In embracing the interconnectedness of pain, we honour the complexity of human life.

We find courage in knowing that our struggles, though challenging, are not endured in solitude.

And in this understanding, we discover the potential for a deeper, more compassionate world where pain is not a barrier but a bridge to the heart of what it means to be human. It's easy for me to sit with my three sisters and reflect of the pains we have had of losing parents sister and brothers it has bonded us and brought us closer, since we have a relatable place of experience of loss, grief and pain. What I have realised over the past years is that it doesn't matter how often you go through deaths of loved ones, you will never be an expert at grieving or get used to deaths of loved ones. The experiences are never the same you discover a knew you all the time on expressing deaths and loss.

The death of my mother during my teenage years was a deeply shattering experience that profoundly disrupted my life. She was the dearest person to me, and I was always her boy. My mother was instrumental in instilling in me the values I hold dear, especially those rooted in faith and Christian principles. Everything I know today about God and prayer was passed down from her teachings and guidance.

Over the years, I've come to understand the importance of identifying the source of one's pain. Knowing where pain originates can be incredibly meaningful, offering clarity and opening a pathway toward healing. By recognizing pain's origins help equips us with the ability in addressing it effectively and understanding its role in our lives. Always take note that, pain plays a very profound good role in our lives.

Physical pain we must understand its basis. How physical pain signals potential or actual damage to the body, prompting a response for protection or healing. It always gives us clues as to what is going on in our emotional space.

It has been proved by medical research that the physical has an impact on mental. It has been highlighted and written on how chronic physical pain can lead to feelings of frustration, hopelessness, and sometimes depression, creating a cycle of suffering.

I speak and write about strategies on how to manage physical pain, based on my own experiences and many others I have spoken to over the years. We have to learn to explore pain management techniques, such as medication, physical therapy, mindfulness practices, eating health, health and wellnesses and the importance of addressing physical pain's emotional effects.

Emotional pain is one of the most challenging experiences we can endure, a universal truth that transcends backgrounds, cultures, and circumstances. It is a deeply human experience, affecting us all in one way or another, and no one is immune to its effects. This kind of pain can stem from various sources—loss, betrayal, rejection, or even the relentless pressures of everyday life. Unlike physical pain, emotional suffering often lingers, leaving scars that can be difficult to heal.

 It can feel isolated, as if we are trapped in our own struggles, unable to communicate the depth of our hurt to those around us.

Yet, it is through these shared experiences of emotional pain that we often find connection and empathy with others, fostering resilience and a greater understanding of the human condition. Acknowledging and confronting this pain is a crucial step in our journey toward healing and personal growth, reminding us that we are not alone in our struggles.

Examining sources of emotional pain, including loss, betrayal, rejection, disappointment, and regret.

a. **The Psychological Impact of Emotional Pain:** Understanding how emotional pain affects self-worth, trust in others, and overall outlook on life.
b. **Coping with Emotional Pain:** The role of self-compassion, support systems, and therapeutic practices (like cognitive-behavioral therapy) in addressing and healing emotional wounds.
c. **Emotional Pain's Role in Growth:** How emotional challenges can lead to increased empathy, resilience, and deeper self-awareness over time.

Spiritual Pain

a. Defining Spiritual Pain: Exploring spiritual pain as a deep feeling of emptiness, disconnection, or questioning of purpose that arises from events that challenge core beliefs or values.
b. Causes of Spiritual Pain: Situations like the death of a loved one, a serious illness, or existential crises that make individuals question life's meaning, purpose, or their relationship with the divine.
c. Signs of Spiritual Distress: Recognizing symptoms such as feelings of abandonment, purposelessness, or being disconnected from oneself or a higher power.
d. Healing Spiritual Pain: Ways to address spiritual pain, including spiritual practices, faith-based communities,

meditative practices, and seeking purpose in service to others.

Spiritual pain often manifests as a profound crisis of meaning and connection, leaving individuals grappling with questions
that challenge their very essence. It can arise during times of loss, personal tragedy, or significant life transitions, prompting an examination of one's beliefs, values, and sense of purpose.

Unlike other forms of pain, spiritual suffering strikes at the core of our existence, leading to feelings of disconnection from oneself, others, and a higher power.

This disconnection can result in an overwhelming sense of emptiness, disillusionment, or even despair, as individuals struggle to find clarity in their lives amidst chaos. During such crises, many seek solace in faith, philosophy, or community, hoping to rediscover a sense of belonging and understanding. While spiritual pain can feel isolated, it also presents an opportunity for profound growth and transformation. By confronting these deep-seated struggles, individuals can cultivate resilience and forge a renewed connection to their beliefs, ultimately leading to a more meaningful and enriched life.

The Interplay Between Physical, Emotional, and Spiritual Pain

The interplays between physical, emotional, and spiritual pain are a complex and intricate relationship that highlights the holistic nature of human suffering. Each type of pain can influence and exacerbate the others, creating a cycle that can be challenging to break. Here are some key points to consider in this interplay:

Mutual Influence: Physical pain often leads to emotional suffering, as chronic discomfort can result in frustration, anxiety, or depression. Conversely, emotional pain, such as grief or trauma can manifest physically through symptoms like fatigue, tension, or unexplained ailments.

Spiritual Disconnection: Experiencing either physical or emotional pain can lead individuals to question their beliefs and purpose, resulting in spiritual pain.

This crisis of meaning can further intensify feelings of hopelessness and despair, complicating the healing process.

Coping Mechanisms: People often seek different coping strategies to manage pain. Physical pain might lead to the use of medication or therapy, while emotional pain might prompt individuals to seek biblical counselling or support groups. Spiritual pain, on the other hand, may drive people to explore their faith or engage in spiritual practices as a means of finding solace.

Holistic Healing: Understanding the interconnectedness of these pain types emphasizes the importance of holistic approaches to healing. Addressing only one aspect of pain may leave others unexamined, whereas a comprehensive approach that incorporates physical, emotional, and spiritual dimensions can lead to more effective healing outcomes.

Empathy and Connection: Recognizing the interplay of pain can foster empathy among individuals experiencing suffering. Sharing experiences and understanding how these forms of pain affect one another can create a sense of community and support, helping individuals feel less isolated in their struggles. Bible based communities with prayerful leaders and believers can help more.

By acknowledging the interplay between physical, emotional, and spiritual pain, we can better understand our own suffering and that of others, paving the way for more compassionate care and a more profound journey toward healing.

Transforming Pain into Insight and Growth

a. Lessons from Each Type of Pain: Recognizing that physical pain builds resilience, emotional pain enhances empathy, and spiritual pain deepens our search for meaning.
b. Seeing Pain as Part of the Human Journey: Understanding that everyone experiences all types of pain, which can build connection, compassion, and insight.
c. Embracing Pain as an Opportunity for Transformation: Accepting pain as a catalyst for personal development, viewing each type of pain as a chapter in life's story that contributes to a fuller, more meaningful life.

By Transforming pain into insight and growth is a profound journey that can lead to personal evolution and resilience. Pain, whether physical, emotional, or spiritual, often serves as a catalyst for change, compelling you to confront your circumstances and seek deeper understanding. This process begins with the acknowledgment of pain, allowing individuals to fully experience their feelings rather than suppress them.

By reflecting on your suffering, one can uncover valuable lessons about themselves and your relationships with others.

As you navigate through the difficult emotions associated with pain, you may discover new strengths, coping mechanisms, and perspectives that were previously hidden from view. This newfound insight can foster a greater sense of empathy, not only towards oneself but also towards others who are suffering. Moreover, as you learn to reframe your pain as a source of growth, you will often cultivate a mindset that embraces challenges as opportunities for development.

Ultimately, the transformation of pain into insight and growth empowers you to rewrite your narratives, shifting from a victim mentality to one of resilience and hope.

This journey can lead you to profound personal transformation, allowing individuals to emerge stronger, more compassionate, and equipped with a clearer sense of purpose. Embracing pain as a teacher can illuminate the path toward healing and self-discovery, creating a richer, more meaningful life experience.

Key Takeaways and Reflections

It (pain) plays a multifaceted role in our lives pain. And by understanding the physical, emotional, and spiritual roots of pain, we can appreciate its complexity and better address it in a holistic manner.

a. Pain has that ability to connect us all. Recognizing how different types of pain influence one another can help us understand our own responses and offer effective support to others.

b. Pain gives us life`s most precious opportunity and that is one to grow. Although pain is challenging, each type offers unique lessons and opportunities for developing resilience, self-awareness, and deeper connections with others and ourselves.

This chapter invites you to deepen your understanding of pain, seeing it not as a burden but as a multifaceted guide on the path of personal growth. Through this exploration, you are empowered to confront and learn from your pain, moving toward healing and a more integrated, meaningful life.

3.
PAIN`S LESSONS, HIDDEN IN SUFFERING

'Every pain gives a lesson, and every lesson
changes a person.'
Unknown

In Pain`s Lessons, Hidden in Suffering, I want you to uncover the valuable insights pain and suffering can offer. Rather than viewing pain merely as an ordeal to endure, this chapter redefines it as a transformative force that, when engaged with mindfully, fosters self-awareness, empathy, and inner strength. Suffering has the potential to teach us about resilience, patience, and our capacity for growth and healing. By looking deeper into our experiences of suffering, readers are encouraged to embrace its lessons, allowing it to refine and shape them in ways that enrich both their inner and outer lives.

Suffering as an encouraging source of growth

Suffering, often perceived solely as a negative experience, can serve as a powerful catalyst for growth and transformation. When faced with challenges, individuals are compelled to confront their limitations, fears, and beliefs, fostering a deeper understanding of themselves. This process can lead to profound insights and personal development. Through suffering, people often discover resilience they never knew they had, learning to navigate difficulties with greater strength and determination.

Moreover, suffering encourages empathy and compassion. Experiencing pain allows individuals to connect with others on a deeper level, understanding the complexities of human experience. This connection often fosters a sense of community, where shared struggles create bonds that uplift and support one another. As individuals work through their suffering, they may also find new perspectives that challenge their previous assumptions about life, instilling a sense of gratitude for the positive aspects that coexist with hardship.

In essence, suffering can be seen as an integral part of the human experience that encourages growth. It invites individuals to reassess their values, priorities, and relationships, often leading to a more profound appreciation for life itself. By embracing suffering as a source of encouragement rather than solely a burden, people can unlock the potential for transformation and emerge from their trials with renewed purpose and strength.

<u>**Some of the unknown gleans on suffering**</u>

These 'gleans' suggesting the precious and valuable takeaways or nuggets of wisdom that arise from painful experiences, even if they are not recognized or acknowledged by everyone.

Essentially, it highlights the notion that through hardship, individuals may discover profound lessons about themselves, their values, and the nature of existence, thus enriching their understanding and experience of life.

a. **Suffering has a role in mankind's experiences.** Recognizing suffering as a universal experience and exploring how it often acts as a pivotal point for self-discovery and growth.

b. We should never waste time fighting suffering but choose to embrace it and learn from it. Learning from it than avoiding pain can prolong suffering, whereas accepting and examining it can reveal hidden lessons and foster resilience.

c. Our view of suffering plays a role in our navigating during that period. We go through what I call, *Transformative Suffering*: It is a viewing of suffering as an opportunity to emerge stronger and more compassionate, rather than as a setback or punishment.

<u>**We grow self -awareness through pain**</u>

History and life have proved beyond any reasonable doubt that pain is not just pain but a mirror. Yes, pain reflects our deepest fears, values, and priorities, allowing us to understand ourselves more fully.

Pain tasks us with the responsibility of identifying unresolved issues be it emotional pain or physical or psychological pain. Recognizing that pain often highlights unresolved emotional wounds, unprocessed feelings, or unmet needs.

One of the beauties of pain is its unmatched ability to help one to develop emotional insight.

Pain can foster a deeper understanding of our emotional responses, helping us become more aware of our triggers, patterns, and sources of inner conflict.

In my being hospitalised and experiencing emotional suffering I have grown in understanding the element of mindfulness through suffering. Through practicing mindfulness with painful experiences can help you and me to observe rather than react, bringing clarity to the underlying emotions and thoughts that drive our suffering.

Self-awareness often emerges from the crucible of pain, serving as a profound teacher that compels us to reflect on our thoughts, emotions, and behaviors. When we encounter challenges or experience suffering, we are pushed to confront aspects of ourselves that we might typically avoid or overlook.

This confrontation can unearth hidden fears, insecurities, and desires, fostering a deeper understanding of our motivations and reactions.

 As we navigate through pain, we begin to discern patterns in our behavior, recognizing how past experiences shape our present selves.

Pain acts as a catalyst for introspection, prompting questions about our identity and purpose. It invites us to examine our relationships, values, and priorities, ultimately leading to greater clarity about who we are and what we truly want from life.

In this process of self-discovery, we learn to cultivate compassion not only for ourselves but also for others who endure similar struggles. Through the lens of pain, we become more attuned to the complexities of human experience, allowing us to develop empathy and a more profound connection with those around us. Ultimately, the journey through pain enriches our self-awareness, enabling us to emerge stronger, more resilient, and with a clearer sense of our place in the world.

Empathy and Compassion are gifts of pain

People who have suffered have a deeper understanding of empathy. Exploring how personal suffering enables us to relate to others' struggles, fostering genuine compassion and the ability to offer meaningful support.

By you and me recognizing the bond that suffering creates, connecting us more deeply to those who have faced similar experiences, and nurturing a sense of shared humanity.

Many have and are learning active compassionate simply because thieve at one point in their lives suffered pain, emotionally or physically so they feel how other feel when they are going through such pains, and they are keen to give help. we use the insights gained from our own suffering to become more patient, understanding, and less judgmental toward others.

Pain is a perfect path leading to forgiveness of oneself and others.

By experiencing suffering can lead to a greater capacity for forgiveness—both of oneself and of others—by helping us understand the complexities and vulnerabilities of the human condition.

Empathy and compassion often blossom from the fertile ground of pain, transforming individual suffering into a powerful connection with others. When we endure hardships, we gain firsthand insight into the struggles that accompany human experience. This personal journey through adversity allows us to understand and relate to the pain of others in a way that is deeply profound. Rather than viewing pain as a solitary burden, we come to recognize it as a shared thread that weaves through the fabric of humanity, uniting us in our vulnerabilities.

As we process our own suffering, we develop a heightened sensitivity to the struggles faced by those around us.

This newfound awareness fosters empathy, enabling us to see beyond superficial differences and connect with others on a fundamental level.

We become more willing to listen, to offer support, and to stand in solidarity with those who are suffering.

Furthermore, compassion, born from our experiences, drives us to take action—whether through acts of kindness, advocacy, or simply being present for someone in need.

In essence, the gifts of empathy and compassion, cultivated through pain, allow us to transform our own experiences into a force for good. They empower us to create a more understanding and caring world, reminding us that through our struggles, we can become beacons of hope and support for others navigating their own challenges. Ultimately, pain does not diminish our capacity for love and connection; instead, it enriches it, reminding us of our shared humanity and the strength we find in compassion.

Applying Suffering's Lessons to Everyday Life

a. Journaling and reflective exercises to help understand and process personal pain, extracting lessons that can guide everyday choices and actions.
b. Practicing gratitude for the growth that pain has fostered, shifting focus from the negative aspects of suffering to the strengths and wisdom it has imparted.
c. Using the insights gained through suffering to make more intentional life choices, align with personal values, and create a life grounded in meaning and purpose.

Transforming Pain into Purpose

a. I encourage readers to use their experiences of suffering as fuel for meaningful pursuits, such as volunteer work, advocacy, or creative projects.
b. Real-life examples of people who transformed their suffering into purposeful actions, finding healing and fulfillment by contributing to causes larger than themselves.

You must grow to inspire other on how personal transformation can serve as a beacon of hope for others, illustrating that while suffering is difficult, it also holds the potential for profound growth and empowerment.

<u>**Takeaways & Reflections**</u>

Key takeaways from the exploration of pain highlight its dual role as both a source of suffering and a catalyst for personal growth. We learn that while pain is an inevitable part of life, it can lead to greater self-awareness, empathy, and resilience.

Each experience of hardship serves as a profound teacher, encouraging us to reflect on our values and priorities.

By embracing our struggles and seeking to understand their lessons, we can transform pain into a powerful force for positive change in ourselves and in the lives of others. Ultimately, these reflections remind us that through our shared experiences of suffering, we can forge deeper connections and foster a more compassionate world.

a. Pain, when embraced, offers invaluable lessons in self-awareness, empathy, and inner strength, shaping us into more compassionate and resilient individuals.
b. By understanding our own suffering, we can relate more deeply to others' experiences, fostering compassion and meaningful connections.
c. Suffering can ultimately serve as a source of strength, driving us to contribute positively to the world and inspire others.

This chapter offers a reimagined view of suffering, encouraging you and me to approach it as an opportunity for growth and self-discovery. By engaging with pain and exploring its hidden lessons, you and me can emerge more self-aware, empathetic, and resilient, carrying these newfound strengths into every aspect of our lives.

4.
THE REALITY OF DEATH
(While bedridden in the hospital)

In this chapter, The Reality of Death (while *bedridden in the hospital*) I explore the profound and often sobering experience of approaching the end of life from a hospital bed. In this chapter, I delve into the physical, emotional, and psychological dimensions of being bedridden and aware of one's face to face with mortality.

In 2021 in Pretoria, I was rushed to Steve Biko Hospital by paramedics who picked me from my flat where I was down and out, couldn't stand, walk or sit. I could hear from a far away tone them talking to each other about my grave condition and the male counterpart was saying to the lady

'We are late we won't make it with him alive to Steve Biko Hospital'

From Madiba Street in central business town in Pretoria it was my longest driver ever in life.

In that fleeting moment, life felt as though it was slipping through my hands—fragile, beyond my control, and leaving me with little more than a desperate grasp at time itself. Staring into the face of death, a profound stillness overcame me, bringing with it an intense clarity about the nature of existence, vulnerability, and surrender.

Each second slowed, revealing truths that are hidden when we are wrapped in the illusion of invincibility.

Confronting mortality, I found myself on the precipice of revelation, a place where life's essence is both raw and unmistakable, where purpose becomes sharper and distractions dissolve. In the presence of such intense vulnerability, I learned that while I could not hold on to life indefinitely, I could transform each moment with the knowledge that it is finite. In this silent understanding, fear began to fade, replaced by a resilience forged in the presence of death's inevitability.

For three long months, I lay hospitalized, caught in a fragile space between life and death. My body was unyielding to treatment, and as days turned to weeks, the doctors' faces grew increasingly solemn. They asked, time and again, if I had provided all my contact details, hinting with each question that they believed the end was near—that I was slipping beyond their reach. In those moments, I could feel their quiet resignation, as if my life had become a ticking clock, its final moments counted out by a force I could neither fight nor understand.

Yet, in this stillness, amidst the despair, I found something unexpected. Facing the reality of my mortality forced me to confront the essence of my existence, and I discovered a resilience within that surprised even me.

Though the medical world had given up, my spirit had not. That liminal space, where all certainty faded, became a place of raw clarity—a realization that, even in surrender, there is strength. In those silent, stark hours. I learned that life, however fleeting, holds a profound, relentless will to endure.

One early morning after my doctor, Professor ____, visited my room, he spoke gravely, listing a cascade of potential illnesses, each more complex than the last. The technical terms blurred together, the implications heavy and beyond my understanding. As he left, I could see the worry etched in my roommate Brother Chris's face. He turned to me, his voice low but earnest, and said *'Herbert, I am afraid for you. Did you hear what the doctor said? We must pray, my brother; it's not looking good for you.'*

In that vulnerable moment, his words brought a profound stillness to the room—a shared recognition of the uncertainty and fragility that hung over me.

The conversation that followed wasn't about despair but about connection, the need for hope, and the strength of shared faith in the face of mounting odds. Through Brother Chris's concern, I found the courage to face what lay ahead, bolstered by the unspoken understanding that I was not alone in my fear, nor in my hope.

Herbert was confined to a wheelchair, unable to leave his bed as pain overtook his every movement, draining his strength and tethering him to a world of physical limitations.

It felt as though life was slipping away, each day marked by the silent agony of enduring yet another hour. But within this place of healing, amidst the uncertainty and vulnerability, he encountered something profound—the transformative power of love.

Through the compassion of caregivers, the support of friends, and the simple acts of kindness that surrounded him, Herbert began to see that love, in all its forms, holds a healing power of its own. It softened the harshness of his pain, bringing warmth where there had only been isolation. In those moments, he discovered that even the most broken spirit could be uplifted by the genuine concern of others, teaching him that love, when shared freely, has the strength to revive even the most weary

Facing Mortality in a Clinical Setting

The hospital environment—surrounded by medical staff, equipment, and routines—can highlight the fragility of life and create a sense of isolation, to cope one has to adjust and embrace the moments.

Reflections on losing the familiar comforts of home and personal autonomy, and how this shift impacts mental and emotional well-being. Exploring the physical discomforts of being bedridden, from immobility to reliance on others for basic needs.

Balancing pain management with alertness and the choices many patients face when changes to being bedridden one needs to adjust while hoping.

Understanding the stages of emotional processing and how each individual experiences them uniquely.

The importance of addressing unresolved emotional wounds, expressing love and forgiveness, and finding closure with oneself and loved ones.

As I lay bedridden, the weight of life and its myriad challenges pressed heavily upon me, yet within that stillness, I found a profound clarity. Each breath became a reminder of the fragility of existence, an acknowledgment that life's most precious moments are often intertwined with pain and uncertainty. The reality of death loomed ever closer, a constant companion that urged me to reflect on what truly mattered. In those quiet hours, I embraced the memories of love, laughter, and connection that filled my life, understanding that these were my greatest treasures. While I may have been physically diminished, my spirit remained unbroken, fueled by a deep appreciation for the journey I had undertaken.

Ultimately, facing the reality of death illuminated the beauty of life, reminding me to cherish each moment, however fleeting, as I prepared to step into the unknown with grace and acceptance.

This chapter encourages you to reflect on mortality, fostering empathy for those bedridden, and highlighting the profound importance of peace and dignity. This is a good time to reflect and make peace.

Through shared reflections and insights, it guides you toward an understanding of how to approach your own difficult moments of not be able to do things but bedridden at the mercy of medical staff.

Facing the reality of death multiple times has imprinted on me the profound awareness that each encounter held a purpose beyond mere survival. There have been more than six moments when I stood at the edge of life, only to be pulled back by an invisible hand, spared not by chance but by a divine decision beyond my comprehension. These experiences taught me that life is not simply extended for its own sake but is preserved with intention, a calling to fulfill the assignments meant uniquely for me.

Each brush with mortality has deepened my understanding of purpose and resilience, fueling my drive to share these stories as a testimony to those who find themselves in their own struggles. I am reminded that while the reality of death is inevitable, the timing of it is held by God alone—a choice that extends our lives not for us to simply exist but to fully live, grow, and impact others.

This has become my motivation: to live a life that honors each day as a gift, embracing each second as a testament to faith, purpose, and the unshakable will to fulfill my calling.

5.

RAVISHED BY DEATH

(Loss of parents, siblings, and loved ones)

1. My First Encounter with Mortality- (my mum`s death)

How the death of a close family member, particularly a parent or sibling, introduces the individual to the reality of mortality. Personal stories or reflections on the initial shock and pain of loss, marking the beginning of a lifelong journey with grief.

My first encounter with mortality was marked by the profound loss of my beloved mother, Betty Mtowo (nee Chideme).

She was the cornerstone of our family—a gracious matriarch who raised not only her nine children but also took in five nieces and nephews, embodying love and selflessness. An Italian-trained cook and baker, she had an angelic voice that could soothe the heaviest of hearts. Losing her during my early teenage years rocked my world and left a void that seemed insurmountable.

77

The experience of her death was my first brush with grief, and for many years, I struggled to comprehend the enormity of that loss. It wasn't until many years later, in 2018, while attending grief support in Springs, Johannesburg, that I began to unravel the emotions tied to her passing. My health had suffered as I grappled with unresolved grief—feelings I had never fully understood or expressed. The pain was not mine alone; it resonated deeply within our family. My brothers and sisters, many of whom were married with families of their own, were equally devastated. Each of us was torn apart by the loss, and I often wondered if there was a single soul among us who emerged unscathed.

One of the most striking memories I hold is of my towering father, a figure of strength and resilience, shedding tears at the loss of his beloved wife. Seeing him vulnerable was a revelation; it reminded me that grief does not discriminate, touching even the strongest of hearts.

To this day, I cherish the fond memories of my mother and often find myself wishing I could have shared my life's journey with her.

She was not just a guiding figure; she was a wellspring of love and wisdom, and her absence left an indelible mark on my spirit. The impact of her death was profound, leading me into a deep reflection on life, loss, and the nature of love.

Yet, amid the darkness, her passing drew me closer to God. Through the biblical teachings she instilled in me, I found a foundation that has anchored my faith throughout the years. Today, I remain firmly rooted in God's word, finding solace and strength in the lessons she imparted.

Her legacy continues to guide me as I navigate life's complexities, reminding me that while pain is an inevitable part of our journey, it can also serve as a pathway to deeper understanding, resilience, and an unwavering faith in the face of adversity.

The first time I witnessed my father cry uncontrollably was a moment etched into my memory forever. It occurred after the death of my mother, Betty Mtowo, a loss that shook our family to its core. As the head of our household, my father had always been the epitome of strength and resilience. He was our protector and our guide, a towering figure who commanded respect and admiration. But in that moment of raw grief, he became a man stripped of his armor, revealing the deep wounds that her passing had inflicted upon him.

For years following her death, my father remained a shadow of the man he once was. He carried the weight of loss with him, as if he had been irrevocably altered by the experience.

His decision never to remarry was a silent testament to the profound sadness that enveloped him; it was as though he had closed the door to love, convinced that no one could ever fill the void left by my mother.

The bond they shared was a rare and beautiful love, and after her death, he seemed to be searching for something that no longer existed.

My father's grief was not just a personal struggle; it permeated our home and shaped the fabric of our family life. He was often withdrawn; caught in a world of memories that he cherished yet found too painful to confront. His laughter became a distant echo, replaced by a solemnity that hung over our household. In many ways, he became a broken man—a shell of the vibrant person he had been before losing his partner. The love and support he had provided to his children were still there, but the light in his eyes had dimmed, leaving us to navigate our own grief alongside his.

As I grew older, I began to understand that my father's tears were not just a reflection of his sorrow but also a poignant expression of love—a love that remained steadfast even in her absence. His mourning was a testament to the depth of their connection, illustrating that true love does not fade away but rather evolves into something different after death. His struggle to cope with her loss served as a reminder of the fragility of life and the importance of cherishing our loved ones while they are with us.

The impact of my mother's death on my father rippled through the years, influencing our family dynamics and shaping our understanding of love and loss. While he remained a loving father, the absence of my mother left a void that was never fully filled.

My father taught me that grief is a journey without a clear destination, and that love can linger long after a person is gone, manifesting itself in memories, tears, and quiet moments of reflection.

In the end, my father's experience illustrated that the death of a beloved partner can profoundly affect not just the individual but the entire family. It is a reminder that while loss can break us, it can also bind us together in shared grief, fostering a deeper appreciation for the love we have and the memories we hold dear. My father's silent suffering and unwavering love for my mother remain an enduring legacy, guiding me as I navigate my own life's challenges and encouraging me to hold tightly to the bonds that define our existence.

Regrettably, I missed my father's death, arriving home only after he had been laid to rest. This absence haunted me for many years, creating a chasm of unresolved emotions that lingered in the background of my life. I felt an overwhelming sense of guilt and heartbreak, knowing that I had not been there to say my final goodbyes or to offer him comfort in his last moments.

The sorrow of not being by his side during such a crucial time weighed heavily on my heart, leaving me with a profound sense of loss that extended beyond his physical departure.

The lack of closure intensified my grief, as I grappled with the memories of my father and the impact of his absence.

I often found myself replaying the moments we shared, wishing I could turn back time to be there for him, to hold his hand as he had once held mine through life's challenges. This internal struggle festered, creating a sense of disconnection not only from my father but also from my own feelings of loss.

It wasn't until I engaged in a thirteen-week grief support program in Springs, Johannesburg, that I began to find a path toward healing. Surrounded by others who had experienced similar losses, I was able to share my story and hear theirs, which created a powerful sense of community and understanding. This process helped me confront my feelings of guilt and regret, allowing me to express emotions that I had kept bottled up for far too long.

Through guided discussions and shared experiences, I learned the importance of acknowledging my pain and recognizing that grief is not a linear journey. I began to understand that it is normal to feel lost and that healing takes time.

Slowly, I started to find closure—not in the traditional sense of having been there at his death, but in the realization that my father's love and memory would always be a part of me.

This support network helped me process my sorrow and come to terms with the fact that while I missed the opportunity to say goodbye, my father would have wanted me to remember him with love rather than regret.

The experience became a catalyst for transformation, allowing me to honor his legacy in my life and instilling in me a deeper appreciation for the fleeting nature of time and relationships.

Ultimately, that grief support journey became a vital chapter in my healing process, enabling me to embrace my father's memory while learning to navigate my own grief with compassion and understanding. Though I may have missed his passing, I found a way to carry him with me in my heart, transforming my pain into a source of strength that continues to guide me through life's challenges.

2. Loosing Parents-Navigating the Absence of a Lifelong Anchor

Understanding the unique grief that follows the loss of a parent, who often serves as a source of support and guidance.

Coping with the 'orphan' feeling, no matter one's age, and the sense of responsibility or loneliness that can arise.
Exploring how this loss can reshape one's identity and lead to a re-evaluation of values and priorities.

The loss of both my parents has profoundly reshaped my understanding of life and identity. Growing up, my parents were not just my caregivers; they were my anchors—steadfast and reliable forces in a world that often felt chaotic and uncertain.
Losing them has been akin to losing the very foundation upon which I built my life. Each of their deaths was a seismic event that rattled my existence, leaving me grappling with the deep void they left behind.

When my mother passed away, I felt an immediate and intense disruption in my life. She had been the heart of our family, nurturing us with love and guidance, and her absence was like a ship adrift at sea, unmoored and vulnerable to the tempests of grief and confusion. Her death forced me to confront my own mortality for the first time, awakening a fear that had previously lay dormant within me. I remember vividly the moments that followed her passing—the disbelief, the anger, and the overwhelming sadness that enveloped my days. It was as if a blanket of darkness had descended upon my world, obscuring the light and joy that once filled it.

My father's death, coming years later, compounded that sense of loss and disorientation. His stoicism and quiet strength had been a source of comfort throughout my life. Witnessing him cry after my mother's death revealed the profound impact her absence had on him, and it shattered my perception of him as an invincible figure.

In his vulnerability, I saw a reflection of my own grief, and I was struck by the realization that even the strongest among us can feel fragile in the face of loss. Losing my father, a man who had been a pillar of strength, left me with an overwhelming sense of isolation. With both parents gone, I felt unmoored, as if I had lost the compass that had always guided me through life's challenges.

The emotional landscape of navigating this absence has been complex. I have grappled with feelings of abandonment, questioning the foundation of love and support I once took for granted. In moments of difficulty, I often find myself reaching out for advice or comfort, only to be reminded that the voices I once relied on are now silent. This realization has been both painful and transformative, pushing me to confront the depths of my grief and to seek new ways of anchoring myself.

In the absence of my parents, I have had to cultivate resilience and self-reliance. Their deaths forced me to draw on the lessons they taught me about strength, perseverance, and the importance of community. I've learned to create my own support system, surrounding myself with friends and mentors who provide guidance and encouragement. This journey has also led me to explore deeper spiritual connections, drawing comfort from my faith and the teachings that have sustained me through dark times.

While the absence of my parents remains a deep ache in my heart, I have discovered that their legacy lives on within me. The values they instilled in me continue to guide my decisions and shape my interactions with others. I carry their memories with me, honoring them by striving to be the kind of person they would be proud of. In this way, I navigate the tides of grief, allowing their love to be a source of strength rather than a reminder of my loss.

Ultimately, losing my parents has been a profound journey of navigating the absence of my lifelong anchors. While the pain of their loss will never fully dissipate, I have learned to find new ways to anchor myself, drawing strength from their memories and the love that endures beyond death. This ongoing journey of healing has transformed my understanding of resilience and the ways we carry the legacies of those we have loved, helping me forge a path forward in a world that often feels uncertain.

The heartache of losing my four brothers' and a young sister

Examining the profound bond between siblings and the lasting impact of losing a brother or sister. The unique grieving process for siblings, who not only lose a loved one but also a shared history and life perspective. How sibling loss can lead you and me to feelings of survivor's guilt, regret, and an amplified sense of one's own mortality.

The pain of losing my siblings—four brothers and a young sister—has etched itself deeply into the fabric of my being. Each of their passing was a unique and devastating blow, one that left an indelible mark on my heart and reshaped my understanding of family, love, and mortality. Among them, my sister Joylene stood out as a beacon of faith, a committed believer who shared a profound bond with me from our earliest days. When she married, however, life took a toll on her spirit. I could see the light dimming in her eyes, and when we finally embraced after years apart, I was overwhelmed by emotion.

The hug that day was a confluence of joy and sorrow, and as I wept uncontrollably, I felt the weight of both our shared faith and the struggles she had endured.

Joylene was the first of my siblings to pass away. Her loss was particularly poignant because it severed a connection that transcended our familial ties; she was a kindred spirit in our devotion to God. Her words still echo in my mind: 'Bhudi Herbert, God is good.' That simple phrase, once a testament to her unwavering faith, became a haunting reminder of her absence. Attending her funeral and burial was a heart-wrenching experience that shattered me in ways I hadn't anticipated. The emotional weight of losing someone who understood my spiritual journey and with whom I shared a unique bond left me feeling profoundly alone.

The grief was palpable, and life felt redesigned to embrace a new reality marked by loneliness and longing.

The subsequent losses of my brothers—Gersham, Rodwell, and Shepherd—only compounded this heartache. Gersham's passing was particularly painful because

I wasn't able to attend his funeral. The last time I had seen him was at our father's burial of; I arrived too late to say goodbye. The regret of not being there to honor his life and legacy gnawed at me. Rodwell's death struck another heavy blow. He was a man of courage and strength, qualities I admired and aspired to embody. His untimely death, like that of my other brothers, felt cruel and unfair.

They had all left this world in their prime, vibrant and full of life, yet death had ravaged them before they could fully realize their potential.

The most shocking loss was that of my big brother Shepherd. Just days before his death, we had spoken on the phone, discussing his desire to visit me in Namibia. When I received the devastating news from my nephew Clive, it felt as though the ground beneath me had vanished. Tears streamed down my face as I processed the reality that another piece of my heart had been torn away. I rushed to catch a flight to attend his funeral, where I was met with a sea of concerned faces. The eyes of those around me spoke volumes, filled with unasked questions and worry about my state of mind. Death had ravaged my life, leaving me grappling with grief that felt unrelenting.

The impact of losing my siblings has been both profound and transformative. Each loss has forced me to confront the fragility of life and the inevitability of death.

I've come to realize that the grief I carry is not just for those I've lost but also for the relationships that will never be fully realized. The void left by their absence is a constant reminder of the love we shared and the moments we will never have again.

In the face of this heartache, I have found solace in the connections I still maintain with those who remain. Ma Tirzah has been a significant source of support through my grief, providing comfort and understanding during my darkest moments.
Her presence in my life has been a balm for my wounds, reminding me that while death takes away, it can also unite us in shared experiences of love and loss.

The deaths of my siblings have profoundly reshaped my perspective on family and relationships. I've learned to cherish every moment with my loved ones, to express my feelings openly, and to seek connection even in times of pain. The heartache of losing them has taught me resilience, empathy, and the importance of carrying their memories with me as I navigate this complex journey of grief. I honor their legacies by striving to live a life that reflects the values and love they instilled in me, ensuring that their spirits remain alive in my heart as I continue to forge ahead in a world forever changed by their absence.

In 2009, just when I thought I might find a semblance of peace after the many storms, tragedy struck again. My only remaining brother, Robson ("Gracious Dad")—passed away.

His passing was compounded by a nearly unimaginable heartbreak; within a short span, both his wife and their 9-month-old daughter passed on as well. The weight of these losses was unbearable. Robson was my last link to the shared history of our family, and his death tore apart the fragile thread of connection I had been holding onto.

At the time, I was leading a team of German experts on a crucial research project, and my supervisor—a German national who valued commitment above all else—insisted I see the project through.

Though I wanted nothing more than to drop everything and be present for my brother's final farewell, I grudgingly agreed to stay. Missing Robson's funeral and burial was devastating; it left me with a gnawing sense of regret that still lingers.

I was only able to attend his memorial service, where I felt the full impact of my absence in the earlier rituals of grief and closure.

This experience underscored how the demands of life can sometimes conflict with our deepest personal needs. The choice to stay was one that haunted me for years. Not being there for Robson's final moments or to comfort our grieving family felt like a betrayal—not just to him, but to myself and the memories we shared.

I came to understand the brutal reality that life often pulls us in directions we least expect, testing our resilience in ways we can hardly bear.

Robson's passing was another defining moment on my journey, a stark reminder of life's fragility and the sacrifices we sometimes make, even unwillingly, as we navigate our commitments and responsibilities. The heartache of missing those final moments with him remains, a painful lesson on the importance of prioritizing loved ones, and it has stayed with me as a somber reminder of the choices we carry through life.

The Complex Layers of Grief

Grieving is a complex journey that often follows five stages: denial, anger, bargaining, depression, and acceptance. These stages aren't a linear path; they can loop back or overlap, surfacing at different times and in unexpected ways. Initially, denial acts as a cushion, helping us to slowly process the reality of loss. As the shock wears off, anger often surfaces, directed at oneself, others, or even at the situation itself. This anger can feel overwhelming but is a natural response to the intense emotions and injustice of loss. Bargaining follows, as we mentally negotiate or revisit past decisions, wishing for a different outcome or clinging to "what if" thoughts.

Depression may then set in, bringing feelings of sadness, emptiness, and isolation. This is a stage of profound sorrow, where the weight of loss becomes more deeply felt.

Eventually, acceptance comes, not as a way of 'moving on' but rather as an acknowledgment of the loss and an ability to move forward with it.

It's also common for grief to show up in ways we might not expect—sometimes as numbness, where emotions feel muted, or even as a sense of relief, especially if the loved one suffered before passing. All these reactions are valid; they're simply part of the unique and personal process of healing through loss. Recognizing the range of emotions in grief helps us to be gentler with ourselves as we navigate the profound impact of loss.

Finding Meaning Amidst Loss

Finding meaning amidst loss is a deeply personal and transformative process. While grief can leave us feeling hollow and disoriented, it also invites us to reflect on what we hold dear and, on the lessons our loved ones imparted. The journey of finding purpose after a loss often starts with a quiet, internal search.

We begin to ask questions about our values, our goals, and what legacies we wish to carry forward.

This process doesn't erase the pain but rather reframes it, helping us to integrate the memories and impact of those we've lost into our lives in a positive way.

In honoring those who have passed, we may find ourselves drawn to actions and decisions that reflect their influence, whether by continuing their work, supporting causes they cared about, or simply living more mindfully. Each small step towards meaning becomes a way to heal, bringing a renewed sense of purpose to our lives.

Loss, though devastating, can thus serve as a catalyst for personal growth, reshaping our priorities and helping us to lead a life that cherishes both the past and the future. Through this journey, we find that while grief may remain, it can coexist with a deeper appreciation for life, connection, and the enduring love that transcends loss.

Coping Mechanisms and Healing Practices

Coping with grief is a multifaceted journey that benefits from a blend of practical strategies and compassionate support. Journaling can serve as a powerful outlet for expressing emotions, providing a safe space to reflect on memories and process difficult feelings. Speaking with a grief counsellor offers guidance and perspective, helping individuals navigate the complex emotions that accompany loss. Support groups, too, are invaluable, offering a sense of shared experience and understanding that reduces isolation.

Engaging in personal rituals of remembrance—such as lighting a candle, visiting a meaningful location, or keeping a loved one's mementos—can help maintain a lasting connection to those who have passed.

Prioritizing self-care is essential in this journey. Regular exercise, a nourishing diet, and adequate rest can all help fortify the body and mind against the physical toll grief often takes. Reaching out to community members, friends, or family for support helps ease the weight of sorrow, reminding us that we don't have to face it alone.
Healing is a gradual process, and these practices offer comfort, grounding, and hope as we rebuild and find balance amidst the pain of loss.

Moving Forward without Moving On

Moving forward without moving on means embracing grief as a part of life that doesn't simply fade away but rather transforms over time.

Instead of "getting over" loss, we carry our loved ones forward in our memories, in the values they taught us, and in the indelible impact they left on our lives. This perspective allows us to honor their presence in meaningful ways, noticing how they live through the choices we make and the person we become.

Acceptance in this context is not about letting go but about integrating the loss into our lives. Over time, grief can become a source of resilience, deepening our compassion and enriching our capacity to support others.

It's a journey that continues, but one that brings growth and enduring connection along the way.

Channeling Loss into Growth

Embrace ways to transform the pain of loss into something meaningful—whether by helping others, honoring loved ones' memories, or making changes that align with the wisdom their lives imparted.

This chapter provides you with understanding, tools, and insights to cope with the death of loved ones, inviting you to find healing and resilience through the pain.
It emphasizes the importance of allowing grief to shape, but not define, one's life.

Takeaways and Reflections

a. Acknowledge that grief is non-linear, deeply personal, and often evolves over time.

b. Each loss and the grieving process that follows is unique and should be approached with self-compassion.

c. Rather than 'letting go,' focus on maintaining a positive connection with those who have passed by cherishing their influence in your life.

God has been my unwavering rock and source of strength through every grief and loss. Without His guidance and the love of compassionate leaders who embraced me in my pain, I would not have found the resilience to endure.

6.
TURNING IT AROUND
(From Victim to Survivor)

In this chapter turning around from –Victim to Survivor, I explore with you the pivotal moment when an individual moves from feeling victimized by their pain to embracing an empowered survivor mindset. This chapter illuminates how recognizing our agency in the face of suffering can lead to transformative empowerment. The journey from victimhood to survivorship involves conscious choices, resilience, and a redefined sense of identity, allowing us to transcend adversity and reclaim control over our lives. Here, you and I are guided to see this turning around not only as a possibility but as a powerful choice that can reshape their entire of one's life experiences.

1. Recognizing the Choice Point

In the depths of grief and loss, we are often confronted with a choice: to remain in the shadows of pain or to find the courage to turn toward life once again. This choice is not an easy one, as it requires confronting deep sorrow and embracing the unknown path ahead. Yet, choosing to live again means honoring both the memory of what we've lost and the strength that lies within us.

It's a decision to move forward—not by forgetting, but by finding a new purpose, allowing the pain to transform us, and making space for joy, healing, and growth.

We have to move from the victim mindsets to survivor mindsets intentionally.

By understanding the difference between seeing oneself as a passive recipient of hardship (victim) and as an active agent of resilience and growth (survivor).

This is easier done through the power of perception. By how we perceive issues it shapes our reality and determines whether we feel trapped by suffering or see it as a stepping stone to strength.

We all have the choices available to us and we must recognize that. Recognizing the moment or moments when we decide to take charge of our healing process, redirecting our energy toward recovery and resilience. Our healing is choice decision away.

2. **From Helplessness to Empowerment-the Journey**

The journey from helplessness to empowerment begins with acknowledging the weight of our struggles and realizing that we hold the power to shape our response. Moving from a place of feeling overwhelmed to a stance of resilience involves small, deliberate steps that rebuild confidence and inner strength. Along this path, we discover our capacity to endure, adapt, and even thrive, using each challenge as a steppingstone. Empowerment comes when we embrace our ability to influence our future, transforming pain into a source of purpose and courage.

Get control and be in charge. The bible says, *'Finally brethren, whatsoever things are true, whatsoever things are honest, whatsoever things are just, whatsoever things are of a good report, if there be any virtue and be any praise think of these things......Philippians 4:8'* our control is mostly over our minds not many things. Understanding that we can't always control what happens to us, but we can control how we respond, and how this shift in mindset restores a sense of autonomy.

Human beings and are driven by beliefs and beliefs can enslave and we have to break free from them. We examine how negative beliefs stemming from suffering can keep us feeling powerless and learning ways to challenge and replace these beliefs.

Healing is your Responsibility.

I tell my clients, friends and family that healing is your responsibility taking responsibility for our healing allows us to move forward constructively, viewing the process as empowering rather than burdensome. Others may have hurt you, yes but healing is something you should be responsible with.

Learn daily to transform your pain into your strengths. By viewing pain not as a detractor but as a catalyst for growth, provides you and me with the strength to face future challenges.

Growing in resilience happens when we learn how to survive these painful experiences.

It is now a known fact that by surviving painful experiences it builds resilience, preparing us to meet life's inevitable difficulties with courage and adaptability.

In life life's flexibility is a must. In life pain is a teacher that fosters flexibility in our responses to life, reducing rigidity and helping us to bounce back more effectively.

Redefining your Life's Identity Beyond Pain

Redefining identity beyond pain involves moving past the hardships that once seemed to define one's self-perception. Instead of allowing pain to remain the core of their identity, individuals can use those experiences to cultivate resilience, empathy, and growth. It's about acknowledging that while pain shapes us, it doesn't have to limit who we become.

This redefinition requires embracing the lessons pain brings without letting it consume our sense of self. By transforming painful experiences into sources of strength, individuals can emerge with a more empowered and holistic understanding of who they are.

Yes, we all understand that while pain shapes our experiences, it does not define our identity. We must grow more into learning to view ourselves as resilient individuals, not as permanent victims.

Crafting a new narrative involves consciously reshaping the story we tell ourselves about our lives and experiences.

By reframing past hardships as opportunities for growth and resilience, individuals can create a more empowering narrative that emphasizes hope and possibility. This process allows one to move forward with intention, embracing a future defined by aspirations rather than limitations imposed by past pain.

Rewriting our story to emphasize growth, resilience, and transformation, shifting from a narrative of suffering to one of empowerment and survival.

Reclaiming purpose and vision in life involves rediscovering the motivations and aspirations that drive us, especially after experiencing loss or trauma. By reflecting on our values and passions, we can realign our goals with what truly matters to us, transforming pain into a powerful catalyst for change.

This reclamation not only ignites a renewed sense of direction but also empowers us to pursue a life filled with meaning and fulfillment ow redefining our identity allows us to connect with a renewed sense of purpose, creating a vision for our future based on strength and resilience.

Embracing a Survivor Mindset-*(Affirmations)*

Embracing a survivor mindset involves cultivating resilience and positivity in the face of adversity.

Here are Four Affirmations to Reinforce this Mindset:

a. I am stronger than my challenges.
b. I choose to learn and grow from my experiences.
c. I have the power to create my own future.
d. My past does not define my present or my potential.

Adopting these affirmations encourages a shift in perspective, allowing us to view obstacles as opportunities for growth rather than insurmountable barriers. This mindset fosters a sense of empowerment, reminding us that we have the inner strength and resources to navigate life's difficulties and emerge victorious. By focusing on our ability to overcome, we can transform pain into purpose and resilience into hope.

How embracing a survivor mindset can positively impact our relationships by fostering self-respect, healthy boundaries, and empathy. Practical tips for sustaining the empowered survivor mindset, even when life presents new difficulties.

Takeaways and Reflections

a. Make the choice to choose to transition from being a victim to a survivor. Recognizing that we have the power to move from feeling victimized by pain to embracing an empowered survivor mentality.
b. Take a new definition of yourself beyond the suffering you have gone through.
c. Understanding that our pain does not define us, and by reclaiming our identity as resilient individuals, we can live a life beyond suffering.
d. Turning around your Pain into life's purposesLearning to use the strength gained from surviving hardships to shape a purposeful and empowered future.

This chapter emphasizes the significance of the turning around point from victimhood to survivorship, encouraging readers to claim their power and rewrite their narrative. By making a conscious choice to grow beyond their suffering, readers can embrace resilience and self-determination, transforming pain into a wellspring of empowerment and purpose

In the journey of life, pain often feels like an uninvited guest, intruding upon our moments of joy and casting a shadow over our hopes. Yet, it is through the crucible of suffering that we can emerge as survivors, transformed by our experiences and equipped with resilience that shapes our character. This chapter explores the profound transition from victimhood to survival, illuminating the path that leads us from despair to empowerment.

Being a victim of circumstances can leave one feeling helpless, as if life is happening to us rather than through us. In the depths of adversity, it is easy to succumb to feelings of powerlessness, allowing our identities to be defined by our suffering. I, too, have wrestled with these feelings.

The loss of my mother, the grief from my brothers' deaths, and the heartache of broken relationships often left me feeling overwhelmed and adrift, like a ship lost at sea.

However, within this tempest of emotions lies a choice: to remain a victim of our circumstances or to rise as a survivor. The transition begins when we acknowledge our pain but refuse to let it define us. It requires us to confront our struggles head-on, to process the hurt, and to seek meaning in the chaos. I learned that while we cannot always control what happens to us, we have the power to choose how we respond.

Through my own journey, I discovered that serving others became a lifeline for my healing. Working with children, particularly those in less privileged circumstances, allowed me to shift my focus away from my pain and redirect it toward something greater. In coaching and mentoring these young lives, I found purpose and fulfillment. Each smile I witnessed and every moment I spent nurturing their potential became a testament to my transformation. The act of giving back not only alleviated my own suffering but also allowed me to cultivate a sense of community and connection.

Survival is not merely about enduring; it is about thriving in the face of adversity. It is about recognizing the strength that arises from our struggles and embracing the lessons learned along the way. In this journey, I encountered many who have walked similar paths—individuals who have faced unimaginable losses yet have emerged stronger, refusing to be defined by their circumstances. Their stories serve as beacons of hope, reminding us that we, too, can reclaim our narratives.

The journey from victim to survivor is a continuous process of growth and self-discovery. It requires courage to face the shadows of our past while moving forward with intention and purpose. We must allow ourselves to grieve, to feel the depths of our emotions, and yet, at the same time, cultivate resilience and hope. It is in this delicate balance that we can transform our pain into a powerful force for change—not only in our lives but also in the lives of those around us.

Ultimately, the path from victim to survivor is not a solitary one. It is a collective journey that connects us to others who share in the human experience of suffering and triumph. In sharing our stories and supporting one another, we create a tapestry of resilience that weaves through the fabric of our lives. Together, we can lift each other from the depths of despair and inspire one another to rise, to thrive, and to become the architects of our destinies.

As we embrace our roles as survivors, we transform our pain into purpose and allow it to fuel our aspirations. Each setback becomes a steppingstone, and each struggle reveals the strength that lies within. In the end, we emerge not just as survivors but as warriors, equipped to face whatever challenges life may throw our way, ready to champion our own narratives and inspire others to do the same.

7.
FACING LIFE`S FEAR OF PAIN

In Facing life`s Fear of Pain, I take you through one of the most significant barriers to healing and growth: the fear of discomfort. Get my other book, I wrote mainly on fear, titled, 'Manage your fear before it's too late 'businesses and life`s opportunities' have been lost simply because we are afraid to try. Let's stick to this chapter in this book though.

In this chapter I explore the instinctive tendency to avoid pain and how this avoidance can prevent us from fully healing and learning from our suffering. By learning to confront and even embrace pain, you and others can cultivate resilience and courage, breaking free from limiting patterns and moving forward with greater clarity and strength. Here, you and others will find strategies to face pain with openness, reframing it as a teacher rather than something to be feared or avoided.

Getting to Grips with the Nature of Fear and Pain

Understanding the nature of fear and pain is essential for personal growth and healing. Fear often serves as a protective mechanism, signaling potential threats and prompting us to take action to safeguard ourselves. However, when fear becomes overwhelming, it can paralyze us, preventing us from pursuing our goals and aspirations.

Pain, both physical and emotional, is an inevitable part of the human experience, and while it can be debilitating, it also has the potential to teach us valuable lessons about our limits and strengths. By confronting and acknowledging our fears and pain, we can learn to navigate them more effectively, ultimately transforming these experiences into opportunities for growth and resilience.

Why as Human Beings Do, We Avoid Discomfort? It is natural instinct by people to avoid pain and society reinforces avoidance through messages of instant gratification and comfort-seeking.

Fear not only paralyses but plays a huge negative impact on healing. That is why many times the fear of pain often contributes negatively more by stalling healing, trapping us in a loop of unresolved emotions and unprocessed experiences.

My dear friend read this again, the best teacher you will ever have and need is **PAIN.** We all on planet earth must come to a place where we learn to view pain not as an enemy, but as an experience that, while uncomfortable, can teach us resilience, self-awareness, and acceptance.

Why is emotional and physical pain consistency, truth be told they are all consistent if they are not addressed. If you don't address it, it won't disappear, and sadly resurfaces in other forms, affecting our mental and physical health, relationships, and overall well-being. Address your pain for your peace and well-being.

There is a price for numbing pain. **DON'T NUMB PAIN!** Examining the effects of numbing techniques, such as substance use, distraction, or emotional detachment, and how these responses ultimately prolong our suffering.

The price of numbing our emotions can be steep, leading to a disconnection from our true selves and our authentic experiences. While it may provide temporary relief from pain, numbing can prevent us from fully engaging with life, hindering our ability to experience joy, love, and connection. This avoidance can result in a build-up of unresolved emotions, which may manifest in more intense emotional or physical symptoms later on. Ultimately, embracing our feelings, even the painful ones, is crucial for personal growth and healing, allowing us to live more fulfilling and meaningful lives.

Sit and Learn from Discomfort

We all have to accept that discomfort is part of life. By us understanding that discomfort is a natural part of growth, will help us to build resilience and a more grounded sense of self.

Sitting with discomfort can be a transformative practice that encourages self-awareness and introspection. By acknowledging our feelings of unease instead of avoiding or suppressing them, we open ourselves up to understanding the root causes of our pain. This process allows us to learn valuable lessons about ourselves, fostering resilience and personal growth.

Ultimately, embracing discomfort can lead to greater emotional intelligence and a deeper connection to our authentic selves.

Strategies to Embrace Pain with Courage

Embracing pain with courage involves acknowledging our suffering and allowing ourselves to feel it fully, rather than avoiding or numbing the experience. Developing a strong support system of friends, family, or professionals can provide the encouragement needed to face our pain head-on. Practicing mindfulness and self-compassion can help us stay present with our emotions, recognizing them as part of the human experience. By reframing pain as a teacher rather than an enemy, we can cultivate resilience and uncover deeper insights that promote healing and personal growth.

Pain is Growth Turned Around

Pain serves as a catalyst for growth by pushing us out of our comfort zones and challenging us to confront our limitations. It often brings hidden strengths and resilience to the surface, revealing our capacity to overcome adversity. Through the process of enduring pain, we gain valuable insights and perspectives that shape our character and enrich our lives. Ultimately, embracing pain as a transformative force allows us to emerge stronger and more aware of our potential for growth. I have grown immensely through my life's struggles and painful moments.

Takeaways and Reflections

a. Don't dodge it but choose to face pain. By choosing to confront rather than avoid pain, we empower ourselves to heal more fully, gain resilience, and break free from cycles of avoidance.
b. Pain contributes to your growths accept it. Embracing discomfort helps us uncover valuable insights, fostering self-acceptance and emotional maturity.
c. Take time to listen to your mind. Learning to sit with discomfort mindfully allows us to process pain in a healthy way, fostering resilience and emotional flexibility.

This chapter guides you in developing a courageous and mindful approach to pain, encouraging them to confront discomfort with openness and acceptance. By shifting from avoidance to acceptance, you can experience a profound transformation, learning to view pain as a teacher that enhances resilience, deepens self-awareness, and enables a balanced approach to life.

8.
BUILD RESILIENCE THROUGH ADVERSITY

'People never cry out to God when there is no pain'
Mathew Hambuda

Since we are all not immune to life's painful moments, I want to share with you how you can build resilience through the same adversities and painful moments you go through or have gone through. Stay put let me take you through. I take you through an exploratory journey on how it can be done. We explore the profound connection between pain and resilience. In this chapter I emphasizes how experiencing and overcoming adversity can fortify our ability to handle future challenges. Resilience is not an innate trait but a skill that can be cultivated through our responses to hardship. By reframing our understanding of pain and viewing it as a source of strength, we can develop endurance and a greater capacity to navigate life's inevitable struggles. This chapter provides insights and strategies to help readers embrace adversity as a catalyst for personal growth and resilience.

Understanding Resilience

Resilience is the ability to adapt, recover, and grow in the face of adversity, trauma, or stress. It involves not just bouncing back from difficult experiences but also developing the capacity to thrive despite challenges. Resilience is not an innate trait; rather, it is a skill that can be cultivated over time through various experiences and intentional practices. It encompasses emotional, mental, and physical aspects, enabling individuals to navigate life's ups and downs effectively.

Resilience comprises several key components, including emotional awareness, optimism, social support, problem-solving skills, and the ability to manage stress. Emotional awareness allows individuals to recognize and understand their feelings, facilitating a more profound connection to their emotions. Optimism is the ability to maintain a hopeful outlook and believe in positive outcomes, even when faced with difficulties. Strong social support networks provide the encouragement and assistance needed during tough times, while problem-solving skills help individuals identify and implement effective solutions to challenges.

Adversity plays a crucial role in the development of resilience. While challenging situations can be painful and distressing, they also provide opportunities for growth and learning. By facing adversity, individuals can discover their strengths, develop coping strategies, and build confidence in their abilities. Resilience is often forged in the crucible of hardship, as people learn to navigate their challenges and emerge with newfound perspectives and capabilities.

Cultivating resilience involves intentional efforts and practices. Mindfulness and self-reflection are vital in helping individuals become more aware of their thoughts and emotions.

Engaging in physical activities, maintaining a healthy lifestyle, and practicing self-care contribute to overall well-being and enhance resilience.

Additionally, developing strong relationships with family, friends, and community can provide a solid support system during difficult times, making it easier to cope with stress and adversity.

Impact of Resilience on Mental Health

Resilience has a significant impact on mental health. Individuals who demonstrate resilience are often better equipped to handle stress and are less likely to experience anxiety or depression in the face of challenges. By fostering a resilient mindset, individuals can learn to approach problems with a constructive attitude, reducing feelings of helplessness and despair. This proactive approach can lead to improved mental health outcomes and a greater sense of overall well-being.

Resilience in Practice

Real-life examples of resilience can be seen in various contexts, from personal experiences to historical events. Individuals who have faced significant hardships—such as illness, loss, or trauma—often share stories of how they adapted and grew stronger through their experiences. Additionally, communities that come together in the face of disaster demonstrate resilience by rebuilding and supporting one another. These stories serve as reminders of the human capacity to overcome adversity and emerge with renewed strength and purpose.

The Lifelong Journey of Resilience

Resilience is not a destination but a lifelong journey. As individuals encounter new challenges throughout their lives, they continue to develop and refine their resilience. Each experience, whether positive or negative, contributes to their overall resilience and understanding of themselves. By embracing the journey and recognizing the value of resilience, individuals can navigate life's uncertainties with greater confidence and determination, fostering a more fulfilling and empowered existence.

The good thing is ppsychological resilience is formed and it can be nurtured through our responses to life's

Your brain is one key component you need to grow in being resilient. By us all knowing how our brains adapt and reorganize in response to stress and adversity, enables our capacity for resilience over time.

Self-Awareness and Reflection: Techniques for cultivating self-awareness to recognize our emotional responses to pain, which is critical for building resilience.

In life be daring take challenges. By playing it safe choosing to stay in the comfort zone won't do you good at all.

The Comfort Zone Paradox: Human beings must understand that by them choosing to stay within their comfort zones can hinder resilience and personal growth, and how stepping outside of them is essential for development.

Takeaways and Reflections

a. Resilience is a skill that can be learned and mastered Resilience can be developed through our responses to pain and adversity, rather than being an inherent trait.
b. By us understanding that facing and overcoming challenges strengthens our endurance and prepares us for future hardships.

This profound chapter empowers you on how to reframe your understanding of pain as a vital component of resilience. By embracing adversity, building endurance, and developing resilience skills, you can transform your experiences of suffering into powerful catalysts for growth, ultimately enhancing your capacity to face future challenges with strength and confidence.

9.
THE GRACE PLACE

*'Our wounds are often the openings into the best and
most beautiful parts of us.'*
David Richo

In life, we all encounter moments of deep sorrow, struggle, and seeming defeat. These are the periods that challenge us beyond what we thought we could bear, moments where pain feels relentless and hope seems distant. In these valleys of suffering, the concept of a "grace place" becomes not just comforting, but essential. This grace place is a state of mind, a heart posture, a spiritual refuge. It's the place within us where we find acceptance, compassion, and strength beyond ourselves — a place we must each find to survive, heal, and ultimately grow from our painful experiences.

Living in the Grace Place

Throughout my life, I have found a constant source of strength, resilience, and peace in what I call '**The grace place.**' It is a space, both internal and spiritual, were pain and hardship become infused with a sense of purpose, strength, and transformation. For many, life's trials can feel like isolating experiences, leaving questions without answers and wounds without healing.

Yet, for me, every hardship — every moment of sickness, loss, struggle, and even the wounds from a painful childhood — has served as an invitation to return to the grace place, where my troubled soul finds a sense of comfort and the strength to carry on.

Growing up, I was the smallest of my siblings. My family lovingly nicknamed me **'Tsidi'** because of my small size, despite being born to parents of considerable stature. My early years were filled with health struggles, including a life-threatening experience during what was meant to be a simple tonsillectomy in the third term of my Grade Five year. I went in for surgery early in the morning, but instead of a quick procedure, I emerged late in the evening, only coming to consciousness several hours later in the evening from a 6:00am surgery, sustained by oxygen support. I had not anticipated that a routine surgery could almost end my life — it was my first lesson in how fragile life could be. Yet, even then, I found myself held by grace, in ways I could not fully understand as a child but sensed deeply.

The grace place has been my foundation, a place I return to when the weight of life becomes too heavy to bear. As a teenager, I faced unspoken battles, carrying the silent pain of being molested during my high school years. The grace place became my sanctuary, even when I couldn't speak openly about my pain until years later when I was lecturing and working in psychology. My survival and growth did not come from ignoring the pain but from learning to meet it in a space of grace.

In this space, I found the courage to face my experiences and to transform them into tools for helping others. For the thousands I have been able to counsel, lead, and teach, it has been this very grace that has enabled me to support them through their darkest moments.

In the grace place, my unanswered questions don't define me.

There are countless things I have endured that remain a mystery — from the early deaths of loved ones to the lingering physical and emotional pain that seemed to accompany me at every stage of life. Yet the grace place has allowed me to sit with these questions without needing answers, to find closure without resolution. Living here has transformed the burden of my losses into a source of compassion and resilience, qualities that allow me to serve others in ways I may never have been able to without my own suffering.

How Pain Became My Teacher

People today look at me and see strength and resilience. They see a person who has achieved academic success, who has found purpose in teaching others, biblical counselling, and helping others. Some are surprised, even baffled, when I tell them that I wasn't always like this. I was never considered particularly bright or strong; my success came through struggles, through the need to work twice as hard as others, both academically and physically, to prove that I was capable.
Each time I was tested, each time I felt the weight of hardship, it was the grace place that strengthened me.

This place of grace has taught me invaluable lessons about humility, about the strength that comes from vulnerability, and about the quiet courage it takes to face life's most painful moments.

Pain has been my teacher, showing me how to approach each day with gratitude and how to see beyond my immediate suffering to the larger purpose of my life.

Each struggle has become a steppingstone, drawing me deeper into the grace place and teaching me how to carry others with me there. It's in this place that I find a wellspring of patience, understanding, and peace — qualities I rely on to guide others through their own suffering.

The Grace Place as a Source of Healing and Transformation

When I speak of the grace place, I'm describing a space where the broken pieces of our lives are gathered, gently mended, and transformed. It is not a place of denial or escape, but one of profound acceptance and renewal. In this place, I've learned that my pain doesn't diminish me; instead, it has become a part of my strength. People often ask me how I have managed to keep going, to endure so much loss and heartache. I tell them that it's because I live in the grace place. Here, my wounds are not signs of defeat but badges of endurance, symbols of a life that continues to grow despite the scars.

The Grace Place Offers Something Invaluable: a lens through which suffering can be reframed as something meaningful. It provides the comfort and closure needed for a troubled soul to heal, to rest, and ultimately to rise again.

In this place, I am reminded that pain, though real and sometimes overwhelming, is temporary.

The impact of grace, however, is enduring. This has allowed me not only to survive my struggles but to turn them into gifts for others.

In my work as a biblical counsellor and teacher, it's this grace that has enabled me to speak from experience, to connect with others on a deeply empathetic level, and to offer hope to those who feel lost in their own pain.

Becoming Whole Through Grace

The grace place has shown me that wholeness is not the absence of struggle, but the presence of a spirit that remains unbroken despite it. It has been the wellspring from which I draw the strength to keep moving forward, even when life seems unbearably heavy. Today, people tell me I am brilliant, resilient, and compassionate. I know that these qualities are not my own but are gifts from the grace place, gifts that were born out of the very pain and struggle that could have broken me.

Living in the grace place has allowed me to redefine my identity beyond my suffering. It has taught me that true strength lies not in avoiding pain but in embracing it, in allowing it to shape me into a more compassionate, resilient, and grounded person.

The grace place is not simply a refuge; it is a space of transformation, a place where pain and purpose meet, where wounds become wisdom, and where brokenness finds healing.

A Life Transformed by Grace

As I continue my journey, I carry the grace place with me as both a reminder and a guide. This space has held me through the most difficult moments of my life and has allowed me to become a source of support for others.

I tell people that I live in the grace place not to suggest that I am without pain, but to show that there is a path through it. Here, I have found my strength, my purpose, and the ability to live a life of meaning, compassion, and service.

The grace place is, in many ways, my life's greatest gift. It is a place of surrender, of healing, and of hope. It has taught me that while pain may be inevitable, grace is always available, ready to transform our deepest suffering into our greatest strength. In the grace place, I am reminded that I am never alone, that my story is one of resilience and growth, and that no matter how difficult the journey, grace will always be there to carry me through.

The Grace of Acceptance

When we enter the grace place, the first thing we find is a gentle invitation to accept what is.

In our pain, it's natural to want to fight, resist, and even deny what has happened. Yet grace brings a shift in perspective. It teaches us that acceptance is not resignation; rather, it is a powerful acknowledgment of reality. Acceptance allows us to pause, to breathe, and to confront our circumstances without being overcome by them.

By accepting, we're not giving up but rather stepping into a space where we can finally begin to heal. This step is crucial because it is often the resistance to pain that deepens it. Grace meets us where we are and gently invites us to release our grip on the "why" and to rest in the "what is."

The Grace of Strength and Resilience

Once we've allowed ourselves to accept our pain, the grace place reveals another gift: resilience. It's easy to think that grace is a passive quality, something soft and unassertive. However, true grace in the face of suffering carries with it a quiet strength. This strength is not rooted in our own abilities but in a deeper well that often feels limitless in moments of trial. Grace gives us permission to be both vulnerable and strong at the same time. We can cry, grieve, and feel the weight of our pain without it defining us or halting our progress. Grace whispers that it's okay to falter, but it also reminds us that we are capable of rising, of pressing on, and of finding light amidst the darkest moments.

This grace-fueled resilience allows us to view our pain through a new lens.
Rather than seeing it as a force that crushes, grace shows us that pain can become a catalyst for growth. When we lean into grace, we discover strength we never knew we possessed. Each step forward, however small, is a testament to this resilience and to the transforming power of grace.

The Grace of Forgiveness and Healing

Another facet of the grace place is forgiveness. Often, our pain is intertwined with wounds inflicted by others or by ourselves. Whether through betrayal, loss, or unmet expectations, our suffering frequently bears the scars of relational wounds.

The grace place is where we find the courage to forgive, not as a means of excusing or forgetting the pain but as a path to freedom. Grace allows us to release the grip of resentment and bitterness, which, if left unaddressed, only intensify our suffering.

In the grace place, forgiveness is not forced or rushed. It is a gentle journey of letting go, of releasing ourselves and others from the burden of past wrongs. This act of grace frees us from carrying the weight of past hurts and opens our hearts to the possibility of healing. Forgiveness does not erase the memory of pain, but it does allow us to move forward without the weight of bitterness dragging us down. Through forgiveness, grace liberates us and makes room for genuine healing to take root.

The Grace of Purpose

Pain, when embraced in the grace place, reveals something profound: purpose. It's common to feel that suffering is random, an unwelcome intruder in the journey of life. Yet grace teaches us that even the darkest chapters hold meaning. As we lean into grace, we begin to see that our struggles often prepare us for something greater. Grace allows us to find meaning in our suffering, to use our experiences as fuel for growth and empathy. Our pain becomes a platform for connection, a way to understand and comfort others who are also suffering.

When we reach the grace place, we find that our pain has shaped us in ways we could never have anticipated. We gain wisdom, strength, and resilience, and these qualities empower us to help others on their journeys. This newfound purpose doesn't erase our pain, but it gives it meaning.

Grace transforms our suffering from a burden into a bridge, connecting us with others and creating a legacy of strength and compassion.

Living in the Grace Place

The grace place is not a destination we reach once and for all; it is a daily choice, a place we return to as life's trials continue to come. It is the quiet retreat we carry within us, the shelter we find when life feels overwhelming. Living in the grace place requires mindfulness, a willingness to sit with our emotions, and the courage to let grace fill our broken spaces.
It's a place we cultivate through prayer, reflection, and seeking connection with others who uplift and inspire us.

In the grace place, we find the courage to let go of the need for answers and to trust in the process. We come to understand that even in pain, we are held, supported, and equipped to move forward.

By choosing grace, we give ourselves permission to feel, to grieve, and to grow without judgment. And with each return to this place, we strengthen our ability to live with both resilience and peace, knowing that we are never truly alone.

Grace does not remove our struggles, but it changes how we experience them. It empowers us to face our pain with courage, to find meaning in hardship, and to discover a resilience we may have never known existed.

In the grace place, we are reminded that pain, however intense, is not the end of our story. It is simply part of a greater journey, one in which grace gives us the strength to not just survive but to thrive.

There are moments when I find myself in rooms, I never imagined I would enter — sitting across from highly accomplished people, working on prominent projects, or entrusted with responsibilities that feel beyond anything I could have orchestrated on my own. Each time I pause to take it all in, I feel a deep sense of awe, and a question lingers: How did I get here? What brought me to this place? In these moments, I know the answer lies in something far greater than my efforts, intelligence, or credentials. I know I am here because of what I call the grace place.

The grace place is not about luck or merit. It's a realm of divine favor, where my weaknesses, shortcomings, and limitations no longer hold me back.

Its where unexpected doors open, where opportunities unfold that defy explanation, and where I experience moments that make me aware of a guiding hand beyond my own. Living in the grace place means knowing that my accomplishments, while real, are not mine alone. I am continuously reminded that this journey is not a result of my own making but of something graciously given, something that lifts me beyond what I could ever have achieved alone.

In the grace place, my life has been filled with 'why me' moments, as I find myself given more than I could have ever earned.

Here, I am reminded that life's true successes are not about being the smartest, strongest, or best-prepared. They come as gifts, moments of grace that carry me to places I never could have anticipated. This awareness not only keeps me humble but also profoundly grateful. Knowing that grace is at work allows me to step into opportunities without fear or insecurity, trusting that I am not there alone, that a larger purpose is at work, and that I am being guided and supported.

Every step in the grace place is a reminder that I don't walk alone, that there is a higher purpose behind each blessing and a reason for every door that opens. It's a powerful realization: I am exactly where I am meant to be, not because of my own merits, but because grace has seen me worthy of this journey.

And with that knowledge, I can walk forward with confidence and peace, knowing that whatever lies ahead, the grace place will continue to be my guide and my anchor.

Living in the grace place is like finding an oasis in the midst of life's most arid deserts. It's where, despite losses and disappointments, I find renewal and strength to keep going. Friendships that I thought would last a lifetime have faded, and hardships have come my way, yet the grace place holds me steady, reminding me that even in pain, there is a greater purpose at work. It's a place of quiet strength where my spirit is fueled, not by pride or anger, but by humility and compassion, knowing that my worth and sustenance do not rely on others or circumstances.

Like Paul's thorn, my struggles keep me grounded, yet in this grace place, I am lifted above the pain, able to see beauty, purpose, and peace beyond what I could ever create on my own. This place is not just my refuge; it's a source of joy and resilience, a reminder that no matter the challenge, I am not defined by hardship but refined through it.

The grace place has shielded me from countless close calls, times when life itself seemed to hang by a thread. I've been through near air disasters, surgeries where I barely made it out, and moments that felt like they'd be my last. I'll never forget a doctor visiting me the morning after a grueling operation, saying with a mix of awe and relief, *'You didn't want to come back.'*

Somehow, against all odds, I did. Though I have faced immense loss, the grace place has given me strength beyond understanding, filling in what was taken with something even greater. It's where life's blessings and trials meet, where I've come to realize that each setback and near-miss has deepened my resilience and heightened my gratitude. In this sacred space, I am continually reminded that grace, not luck, has carried me this far, and I am more whole for every challenge endured.

10.
THE SUN WILL RISE AGAIN

In the darkest hours of my life, I have clung to the belief that my story is far from over. There's a resilience in the soul of those who have known loss, hardship, and pain—a quiet, fierce hope that whispers, *'The sun will rise again.'* This belief has carried me through some of my lowest points. When grief threatens to engulf you, when setbacks seem insurmountable, hope is that single thread you hold on to, trusting that dawn will break on the other side of this seemingly endless night.

Life's journey, for all its beauty, has a way of humbling us with unexpected trials. I've faced years marked by profound losses and challenges, days where it felt nearly impossible to get up and try again. Yet somehow, I would find myself whispering, *'Tomorrow, I'll try once more.'* This resilience—this commitment to persevere despite the circumstances—is what champions understand deeply. A true champion is not only defined by victory but by the resolve to rise after every defeat, bruised but unbowed, knowing that trying again is itself a mark of strength.

One of life's hardest lessons is that we do not always get immediate rewards for our endurance. Often, there are seasons where we walk through the shadows, our path barely visible, uncertain and afraid. But in these times, we cultivate patience, trust, and a kind of faith that cannot be shaken. It is a faith that says, 'Even though I cannot see what lies ahead, I believe that the light will find me.'
This is the essence of hope: it is not blind optimism, but a conviction that there is purpose beyond pain, and that better days are within reach.

'The sun will rise again' is more than a hopeful saying; it is a promise woven into the fabric of existence. Just as night always yields to morning, our challenges contain within them the seeds of transformation. Each time the sun rises, it signals a new beginning, a fresh opportunity to try, to hope, and to live fully. Our journey may be fraught with setbacks and heartache, but each dawn reminds us that life moves forward, and so must we.

For anyone facing immense challenges, remember that hope is a choice—a powerful declaration that our story is not done. Champions know that setbacks do not define us; rather, it's our response to them that shapes our lives. We might not always feel strong, but strength isn't about never falling; it's about rising again and again. When life feels too heavy, remember that better days are coming. Stand firm in the knowledge that, though the road may be rough, the dawn will break, and the sun will indeed rise again.

11.
HOPE IS A CHOICE

In the midst of life's most grueling seasons, when pain overwhelms and hope seems a distant memory, there exists a powerful, quiet choice we can make. This choice—to hold onto hope despite the darkness—is often one of the hardest decisions we face. Yet hope is not a fleeting feeling or a product of circumstance; it is a deliberate act of will. When we choose hope, we commit to believing in the possibility of something better, even when nothing in our present situation seems to support it. And in choosing hope, we open ourselves to the strength needed to endure, to find meaning in pain, and to continue forward.

The moments that truly test us are the ones that seem insurmountable. Pain has a way of shrinking our world, blinding us to anything beyond immediate anguish. In these times, it can be easy to surrender, to let ourselves feel defeated. But hope calls us to look up, to see beyond our suffering even if only a little. Choosing hope means acknowledging that this chapter is not the entire story. It means trusting that there is something beyond the hardship we're facing, that life has greater moments yet to come.

Hope gives us the courage to believe in the possibility of healing and new beginnings.

Choosing hope is not a denial of pain or a way to minimize the reality of our suffering. Rather, it is an acceptance that while pain is present, it does not have the final word. By embracing hope, we create a space within ourselves where possibilities can exist alongside our struggles.

We choose not to let our hurt define us, nor to become prisoners of despair.

Hope is a declaration that, even in our brokenness, we are open to the potential for restoration, for light to enter the cracks of our wounded hearts. This choice honors both our pain and our resilience.

Hope is also a choice that grows with practice. Each time we decide to be hopeful, even in small ways, we build the strength to choose it again. Perhaps today, it's the decision to get out of bed when we'd rather hide away. Tomorrow, it might mean reaching out to someone, seeking support, or daring to dream again. These moments may seem insignificant, but they represent our commitment to living fully despite life's hardships. Over time, these small acts of hope accumulate, giving us a sense of purpose and the knowledge that we can endure.

Ultimately, hope is a powerful declaration of life's worth. When we choose hope, we affirm that the journey, with all its ups and downs, is worth continuing. We may not know what lies ahead, and we may stumble along the way, but hope sustains us, giving us a reason to rise each morning and a faith that our story is still unfolding. In this way, hope is a radical act—a refusal to be conquered by life's pain, a decision to keep going even when all seems lost.

And as we walk this path, we realize that, though we are taught and shaped by pain, hope is our choice and our guiding light.

Hope is a lifeline in the storm, a compass pointing us toward a future we can't yet see. When we face the darkest of moments, like deep relationship breakups, setbacks, or those 'ugly spanners' that life throws our way, hope is often the only thing that keeps us from sinking. It fuels the belief that even though we may feel down, we are not out, and that we still have a fight left within us.

Hope allows us to see past the pain, holding on to the possibility of a brighter tomorrow even when today feels unbearable. It says, *'Yes, this is hard, but it's not the end.'*

God calls us to hope in Him precisely because He understands the valleys we'll encounter. He knows that life can dim even the strongest spirits, that there will be times when we feel empty, clinging to nothing but the "thin air" of a small whisper telling us to keep going. God's promise and presence become our anchor when our strength wanes, providing a steadfast reason to hold on. This divine hope reminds us that while our understanding and resilience may waver, His purpose and vision for our lives remain intact. Hope in God gives us an unshakable foundation—a reminder that, in His hands, no trial is wasted, and no setback is permanent.

Hope is an essential fuel in life's journey; it's what sustains us as we start new ventures, build our dreams, and recover from setbacks.
Without it, we risk losing the motivation to push forward. Look at Joseph: locked away in a dungeon, with every reason to believe that his dreams of greatness were gone forever.

Yet he held on to a small glimmer of hope—a belief that the promise over his life would come to pass. It was that tiny seed of hope that broke the walls of his prison, bringing his fleeting dreams into reality. Like Joseph, if we lose hope, we risk sabotaging our future, denying the world the greatness within us that only hope can bring out.

I've lived on both sides of this divide, having faced moments of hopelessness where I thought everything was over. But even then, there was always a small voice—whispering, nudging, urging me not to give up, telling me, *'Herbert, you aren't done yet.'* That voice of hope has been a constant, showing me time and time again that there's still more to my story. In life's most painful moments, hope acts as our inner guide, urging us to keep moving forward. It transforms pain into resilience, dreams into reality, and despair into purpose.

We need hope to accomplish what we're meant to build; it is, and will always be, the light we need to see us through the dark.

Hope is God's quiet but powerful voice, urging us to press on even when the path is unclear. It whispers that there is purpose in our pain and beauty beyond our struggle. Through hope, we hear His promise that the story isn't over yet—there's more to live, more to become, and more to give.

12.
FORGIVENESS` ROLE IN HEALING

In The Role of Forgiveness in Healing, we explore the profound impact that forgiveness can have on our emotional and psychological well-being. Forgiveness is often seen as a difficult and complex process, but it is a crucial step in alleviating pain and fostering healing. This chapter delves into the nature of forgiveness, the barriers that prevent us from forgiving, and the transformative power of letting go of grudges and resentment. By learning to forgive ourselves and others, we can pave the way for deeper emotional healing, personal growth, and renewed connections with ourselves and those around us.

Forgiveness is the essential doorway to healing from life's pains, disappointments, and rejections. When we forgive those who have hurt us—even if they've never asked for it or are no longer here to hear it—we release ourselves from the grip of bitterness and resentment. Forgiveness is not a simple act or a moment; it's a process that unfolds over time, one that allows us to gradually shed the weight of anger and toxic emotions that would otherwise drain our joy and sap our potential.

Learning to forgive those who have inflicted deep wounds is no easy task, especially when the scars linger and memories replay. However, choosing to forgive, even grudgingly at first, is a choice for our own peace and future. It's acknowledging that our well-being is worth more than the hold of past hurts.

By forgiving, we transform our painful memories into steppingstones for growth rather than roadblocks.

Forgiveness brings healing that radiates through our entire being. It softens the bitterness in our hearts, frees us from the destructive power of anger, and opens us up to receive life's blessings again. When we ask God to guide us through this journey, He provides the grace to forgive, no matter how difficult it seems. In doing so, we elevate ourselves, gaining clarity, renewed strength, and a profound peace that only forgiveness can bring. True healing begins when we let go, trusting that this choice is not about forgetting the pain but choosing to rise above it and move forward.

Understanding Forgiveness

Forgiveness is the conscious decision to release feelings of resentment or vengeance toward someone who has harmed you, regardless of whether they deserve it or ask for it. It is an active process that involves letting go of past hurt, allowing for healing and personal growth, ultimately freeing oneself from the emotional burdens that can hinder well-being. Exploring what forgiveness really means—not condoning wrongdoing but releasing the grip of resentment and anger.

The psychology of forgiveness

The psychology of forgiveness involves understanding that holding onto anger and resentment can negatively impact our mental and emotional health.

Forgiving someone doesn't mean condoning their actions; instead, it's about freeing ourselves from the emotional weight that their actions may have caused us. By choosing to forgive, we can improve our well-being, reduce stress, and open ourselves up to healthier relationships and personal growth. Understanding the psychological mechanisms involved in forgiveness, including emotional release and cognitive restructuring.

Forgiveness vs. Reconciliation

Differentiating between forgiveness and reconciliation; forgiveness can occur without restoring a relationship. Forgiveness and reconciliation are distinct processes; forgiveness involves letting go of resentment and anger towards someone who has hurt us, while reconciliation aims to restore the broken relationship. It's possible to genuinely forgive someone without reconciling because forgiveness is primarily about our own healing and emotional well-being.

In some cases, the relationship may not be healthy or safe to restore but choosing to forgive allows us to release the burden of negativity and move forward. Ultimately, forgiveness is a personal choice that can lead to inner peace, regardless of whether the relationship is repaired.

Restoration after forgiveness is a delicate process that often requires guidance from a mature or professional mediator to navigate the complexities of emotions involved.

When individuals choose to forgive but also wish to reconcile, it's essential to address the underlying issues that caused the rift in the first place. This means engaging in open and honest communication, where both parties can express their feelings and concerns in a safe environment.

Biblical Counselling can provide a structured framework for this dialogue, helping individuals to develop the necessary skills to understand each other better and rebuild trust. Without this guidance, even well-intentioned efforts at reconciliation can lead to misunderstandings and unresolved tensions, which can exacerbate past hurts. In extreme cases, such unresolved issues can escalate into violent reactions, as individuals may still be grappling with anger or pain that hasn't been properly addressed.

Thus, professional support not only facilitates healing but also helps prevent potential conflicts, allowing the relationship to develop on a healthier foundation.

Myths around forgiveness

Myths surrounding forgiveness often create misconceptions that can hinder personal healing and growth. One common myth is that forgiving someone means condoning their actions, which can lead to the belief that forgiveness is a sign of weakness or cowardice. In reality, forgiveness is a powerful act of reclaiming one's own peace and moving forward from the pain inflicted by others.

Another prevalent myth is that forgiveness is an instantaneous event rather than a process; many people believe that simply saying 'I forgive you' is enough to erase the hurt. This misunderstanding can result in frustration when individuals find themselves still grappling with their emotions long after they have attempted to forgive. Additionally, there's a notion that forgiveness requires reconciliation, leading some to avoid forgiveness altogether to protect themselves from further harm.

Some believe that forgiveness means letting go of the memory of the offense, but true forgiveness often involves acknowledging the pain and learning from it. Lastly, the idea that forgiving someone means you have to trust them again can prevent individuals from embracing forgiveness, as they fear being hurt once more. By debunking these myths, we can better understand that forgiveness is a courageous and transformative choice that empowers us to heal and grow.

Known benefits of Forgiveness for the Victim(hurt)

Forgiveness can be a transformative process for victims, offering numerous benefits that contribute to emotional and psychological well-being.

<u>Some core benefits of forgiveness for the hurt person:</u>

a. **Emotional Liberation:** Forgiveness frees individuals from the heavy burden of anger, resentment, and bitterness. By letting go of these negative emotions, victims can experience a profound sense of relief and liberation, allowing them to move forward without being weighed down by past grievances.

b. **Empowerment:** Choosing to forgive is an empowering act that puts the control back in the hands of the victim. Rather than allowing the hurtful actions of others to dictate their emotional state, individuals reclaim their power, fostering a sense of agency over their own healing journey.

c. **Personal Growth:** The process of forgiveness encourages introspection and self-reflection. It often leads to greater self-awareness and personal growth, as individuals confront their feelings, understand their triggers, and learn valuable lessons about themselves and their relationships.

d. **Emotional Stability:** Holding onto grudges and unresolved conflict can lead to chronic stress and emotional instability. Forgiveness promotes emotional stability by reducing anxiety and fostering a more balanced state of mind, ultimately contributing to better mental health.

e. **Peace of Mind:** Achieving forgiveness can create a profound sense of inner peace. This tranquility is invaluable and cannot be purchased; it arises from the realization that the past does not have to define one's present or future, allowing individuals to focus on the positive aspects of their lives.

f. **Improved Relationships:** While forgiveness does not always require reconciliation, it can lead to healthier interactions with others. By letting go of resentment, individuals may find themselves more open to rebuilding relationships or establishing new connections based on trust and understanding, ultimately enhancing their social support systems. people who have not forgiven struggle to love and trust.

In essence, forgiveness is a gift that victims give to themselves, unlocking a pathway to healing, growth, and a brighter future.

Physical Health Benefits: Exploring research that connects forgiveness with better physical health, including lower blood pressure and improved heart health.

Forgiveness offers a range of significant physical health benefits that can enhance overall well-being. Research has shown that letting go of grudges and resentment can lead to reduced stress levels, which in turn lowers the risk of stress-related illnesses such as hypertension and cardiovascular disease. Individuals who practice forgiveness often experience improved immune function, allowing their bodies to better fend off illness and infection.

Additionally, forgiveness can lead to better sleep quality, as individuals are less likely to ruminate on negative experiences or feelings of anger before bedtime. Those who embrace forgiveness also report experiencing less chronic pain, as the emotional burden of holding onto grudges can manifest physically. Ultimately, the act of forgiving can lead to a healthier, more balanced lifestyle, fostering both emotional and physical vitality.

Take note that, forgiveness can mend relationships and create a foundation for healthier interactions and communication.

The Barriers to Forgiveness

a. **The Grievance Cycle**
The grievance cycle can create significant barriers to forgiveness, often perpetuating feelings of resentment and anger. When individuals become trapped in this cycle, they may repeatedly relive their pain, which reinforces

their emotional wounds and hinders their ability to move forward. Additionally, the desire for retribution or the need to feel justified in their anger can further entrench them in the cycle, making forgiveness seem unattainable. Breaking free from this cycle requires conscious effort and a willingness to challenge the narratives that keep one stuck in grievance, allowing space for healing and the possibility of forgiveness. Understanding how holding onto grudges perpetuates a cycle of pain and prevents healing.

b. Fear of Vulnerability

Exploring how fear of being hurt again can make it difficult to forgive and open oneself up to future relationships. The fear of vulnerability can be a significant barrier to forgiveness, as it often prevents individuals from opening themselves up to the possibility of reconciliation and healing. This fear can stem from past experiences where being vulnerable led to pain or betrayal, causing a person to build emotional walls to protect themselves.

Consequently, this self-imposed isolation can cost them valuable relationships and life's precious opportunities, as it fosters a mindset of mistrust and defensiveness.

By holding onto resentment and refusing to forgive, individuals not only miss out on the chance to heal their wounds but also risk losing connections with others who could provide support, understanding, and love.

Embracing vulnerability, while challenging, can ultimately lead to deeper, more meaningful relationships and a more fulfilling life.

c. Desire for Revenge (retribution)

It's a human nature to want to revenge always. The desire for revenge can serve as a formidable barrier to forgiveness, often consuming individuals with thoughts of retribution rather than healing. This yearning to 'get even' can provide a temporary sense of satisfaction but ultimately keeps one trapped in a cycle of anger and negativity, hindering emotional growth. Holding onto the need for vengeance prevents individuals from moving forward, as their focus remains fixed on the past and the perceived injustices they have suffered. This desire can also cloud judgment, leading to decisions that may escalate conflict rather than resolve it, further entrenching the hurt and resentment.

Instead of fostering forgiveness, the pursuit of revenge often exacerbates emotional pain and prevents the possibility of reconciliation, making it essential to recognize and address these feelings to pave the way for healing and peace.

Ultimately, letting go of the desire for revenge allows individuals to reclaim their power and redirect their energy towards personal growth and emotional well-being.

d. Self-Forgiveness Obstacles

Self-forgiveness obstacles often stem from deep-seated guilt and shame, which can create a mental barrier to accepting one's flaws and mistakes. Many individuals struggle to forgive themselves because they believe they do not deserve forgiveness, leading to a cycle of self-blame that hinders emotional healing and personal growth.

Additionally, societal expectations and internalized criticism can exacerbate these feelings, making it challenging to embrace self-compassion and acknowledge that everyone is capable of making errors and learning from them.

The Process of Forgiveness

The process of forgiveness can be broken down into five simple steps and I have used these were used in my own life by those who took me through the journey of forgiveness, and I have also them with my clients, glad they are applicable to anyone.

a. **Acknowledge the Hurt:** Take time to recognize and accept the pain you feel. Understanding the impact of the hurt is the first step toward healing.
b. **Reflect on the Situation**: Think about what happened and why it hurt you. Consider the context and the other person's perspective, which can help you gain insight and empathy.
c. **Decide to Forgive:** Make a conscious decision to forgive. This doesn't mean you condone what happened, but you choose to let go of the anger and resentment for your own peace of mind.
d. **Express your Feelings:** Share your thoughts and feelings about the situation, either with the person who hurt you or through journaling. This will help you process your emotions and reinforce your decision to forgive. The empty chair therapeutic session is a powerful technique often used in counselling to help individuals express their feelings and thoughts about unresolved issues or relationships. In this exercise, a person imagines that someone they need to confront or forgive is sitting in an empty chair across from them.

They are encouraged to openly communicate their emotions, whether it be anger, sadness, or forgiveness, as if that person were actually present. This process allows for catharsis, promotes emotional release, and helps individuals gain clarity and closure by voicing their feelings in a safe and controlled environment.

e. **Release and Move On**: Let go of the negative feelings associated with the hurt. Focus on your own growth and healing, and try to cultivate positive emotions, knowing that forgiveness is a journey that benefits you.

Self-forgiveness is a Catalyst to Healing

Self-forgiveness involves acknowledging one's mistakes or shortcomings, understanding the impact of those actions, and allowing oneself the grace to move forward without being held captive by guilt or shame. It is not merely a result-driven process but rather a transformative journey that fosters personal growth and emotional well-being. Self-forgiveness entails recognizing that everyone makes mistakes and that these do not define our worth or potential.

It encourages individuals to reflect on their experiences, learn from them, and commit to making better choices in the future. Ultimately, self-forgiveness is about cultivating compassion for oneself, leading to healing and the ability to embrace life anew.

Key Points

a. **Acknowledge your Mistakes**: Point out your mistakes don't keep playing the victim game and by recognizing g and accepting the wrongdoings is the first step toward self-forgiveness.
b. **Your Emotional Release is Important**: Allowing oneself to feel and express emotions related to guilt or shame is crucial in the healing process.
c. **Learn and Grow:** View your mistakes as opportunities for learning it fosters resilience and personal development.

d. **Do Self-compassionate Talks:** Be responsible in replacing negative self-criticism with kind and understanding dialogue which enhance self-forgiveness.

Your Path Toward Healing Through Forgiveness

a. **Forgiveness is always Choice:** in your mind reinforces the understanding that forgiveness is an active decision, not a passive emotion, empowering readers to take control of their healing journey.
b. **Move forward**: This is self-intentional step after forgiveness. Discuss how you are going to create a positive path forward after forgiving, including setting boundaries and focusing on future goals.

Healing through forgiveness is a profound journey that requires patience and self-compassion.

By actively choosing to let go of grudges, you create space for emotional freedom and peace in your life. This path encourages you to acknowledge your pain while also recognizing the power of forgiveness to transform your experiences. Ultimately, embracing forgiveness can lead to renewed hope, stronger relationships, and a more resilient

Takeaways & Reflections

a. **Emphasizing** that forgiveness is not about excusing wrongs but about liberating ourselves from the burdens of anger and resentment.
b. **The Dual Journey of Forgiveness**: Understanding that the journey of forgiveness encompasses both forgiving others and ourselves, leading to holistic healing.
c. **Recognize** that choosing to forgive is a powerful act of agency, fostering emotional freedom and resilience.

My life underwent a profound transformation the moment I embraced the journey of forgiveness, despite the immense weight of the hurts I had endured. For a long time, I carried the burden of shame associated with the experiences that had shaped me. The feelings of humiliation and injustice loomed large, fueled by the distorted narratives that others spun about my situation. However, as I stepped onto the path of forgiveness, I discovered a sense of liberation that I had never known before.

Forgiveness became a powerful tool for reclaiming my peace. It allowed me to let go of the anger and resentment that had held me captive for so long. I realized that my healing was not contingent upon anyone else's understanding or validation of my experiences. I no longer felt the need to justify myself or explain the truth behind the hurt to others, especially those who had twisted the facts for their own narratives.

Instead, I found solace in knowing that I was taking control of my own story, defining my narrative on my own terms.

This journey wasn't easy; it required me to confront painful memories and the emotions that accompanied them. Yet, with each step I took towards forgiveness, I felt a weight lifted off my shoulders.

I learned that forgiveness doesn't mean condoning the actions of those who hurt me; rather, it is a conscious choice to release myself from the chains of bitterness and resentment. By choosing to forgive, I found a newfound strength within myself, empowering me to move forward without the emotional baggage of my past.

The peace I discovered through forgiveness was profound. It provided me with a quiet assurance that I could navigate life's challenges without being haunted by old wounds. I began to appreciate the beauty of living in the present moment, free from the shadows of my past. This peace transformed my perspective, allowing me to focus on the future with hope and positivity.

Ultimately, my journey of forgiveness has not only changed my life; it has redefined who I am. I have become more resilient, compassionate, and understanding. I no longer allow the hurt of others to dictate my happiness.

Instead, I cherish the strength I have gained and the lessons I have learned.

Walking the path of forgiveness has truly been a journey of empowerment, leading me to a life filled with peace, purpose, and the unwavering belief that I am capable of overcoming any adversity.

This chapter empowers you to embrace forgiveness as a transformative tool for healing. By understanding the complexities of forgiveness, confronting barriers, and actively engaging in the process, you can experience profound emotional relief and cultivate a more compassionate and fulfilling life. Through forgiveness, we open the door to healing, connection, and personal growth.

13.
GOD'S PRESENCE IN OUR PAIN

Pain has a unique way of making us feel isolated and abandoned, as though we are left to endure hardship without support. In these moments, it can seem like God is distant or silent. Even Jesus, in His moment of anguish on the cross, cried out, *'My God, My God, why have You forsaken Me?'* (Matthew 27:46). This deep human cry captures what so many of us feel during our darkest hours. Yet, through Scripture and the lives of faithful believers, we find that God's presence is steadfast even in the depths of our suffering. While the pain may blur our perception of His presence, God is, in fact, closest to us in these vulnerable moments.

God's promise of companionship is woven throughout the Bible, affirming that we are never truly alone. In Isaiah 41:10, He says, *'Fear not, for I am with you; be not dismayed, for I am your God. I will strengthen you; I will help you; I will uphold you with my righteous right hand.'* This verse is a powerful reminder that God's support and strength are ever-present.

When we're weighed down by hardship, His presence acts as a solid foundation, offering us the resilience and peace we cannot find on our own.

The Psalmist also reminds us in Psalm 34:18 that *'The Lord is close to the broken-hearted and saves those who are crushed in spirit.'* God's closeness is not a far-off concept; it is an active, comforting embrace that shields us, especially when we are most fragile.

Our faith assures us that our struggles are not purposeless. Romans 8:28 reminds us that *'We know that in all things God works for the good of those who love him, who have been called according to his purpose.'* This verse doesn't imply that God causes our pain, but rather that He can redeem it, bringing growth and purpose out of suffering.

Through trials, we often gain spiritual insight, empathy for others, and a stronger relationship with God. When we lean on Him in times of trouble, our trust deepens, and we learn to find comfort in His presence, knowing that He sees and understands our pain in ways we may never fully grasp.

Embracing God's presence during life's lowest times is an act of faith that opens us to His transformative love. It is through our rawest experiences that God shapes us, drawing us nearer to His heart. Hebrews 13:5 reminds us, *'I will never leave you nor forsake you.'* These words are a solemn promise that, no matter what we endure, we do not face it alone. As we rest in God's assurance, we can find peace even in the midst of suffering, knowing that.

His presence fills the void of our pain, turning moments of despair into sacred encounters with His grace and strength.

In this place of divine companionship, we are never forsaken.

14.
TURNING ANGER AND GRIEF INTO PURPOSE
(Transformational)

By turning Anger and Grief into Purpose, in this chapter, which is transformational, I take you through the powerful process of channeling intense emotions—specifically anger and grief—into constructive actions and meaningful goals. While these emotions can often feel overwhelming and debilitating, they also hold the potential to inspire significant personal growth and transformation. This chapter explores how acknowledging, processing, and ultimately transforming these emotions can lead individuals toward a renewed sense of purpose, motivation, and clarity in their lives. Through various strategies and real-life examples, readers will learn how to harness their emotional experiences as a catalyst for positive change.

Grief and anger are deeply personal and often overwhelming emotions that can arise after a significant loss or painful experience. While these feelings may initially seem like insurmountable obstacles, they can also be catalysts for profound transformation. It's natural to feel anger at the injustice or unfairness of certain situations, and grief can create a sense of emptiness that feels impossible to fill. Yet rather than allowing these emotions to consume us, many find that they can channel their anger and grief into meaningful action.

When approached with intentionality, this process can become a way of honoring what we've lost, finding purpose beyond the pain, and ultimately fostering personal growth.

Transforming anger into purpose requires recognizing that anger, while painful, often reveals what matters most to us. For many, the root of anger is love—whether for people, values, or ideals. Anger surfaces because something precious has been taken away or threatened. By exploring what lies beneath the anger, we can begin to understand what we truly cherish. From this clarity, we gain direction for positive change. For instance, someone who loses a loved one to illness might channel their anger into advocacy for better healthcare or fundraising for medical research. In this way, anger becomes a motivating force, driving action that can make a difference.

Grief, too, has a transformative potential that often goes unrecognized. While grief may initially feel like a void, it can also create space for new perspectives and purpose. Grieving allows us to reflect on what has been lost, why it mattered, and how we can honor it moving forward. This reflection can lead to personal and spiritual growth, giving us a sense of clarity and appreciation for life's fragility.

Instead of viewing grief as something to overcome, it can be embraced as part of the healing process, one that reshapes us and opens us to deeper understanding and empathy. Many people have discovered their life's work or calling after enduring a significant loss.

Turning pain into purpose is also an act of self-compassion. It acknowledges that pain is real and deserves recognition. In pursuing a purpose that stems from grief or anger, we are caring for our own emotional well-being, allowing ourselves to process and express what we feel in constructive ways. Purpose-driven actions, even small ones, can create moments of relief and help us regain a sense of agency. By setting goals and taking small steps, we reclaim a sense of control over our lives, which can be especially empowering in the face of loss that often feels out of our hands. In this way, purpose is a bridge from helplessness to hope.

Community involvement can also be a powerful outlet for transforming anger and grief into purpose. When we share our experiences, we realize that we are not alone; there are others who are struggling and who understand our pain. Whether through volunteer work, joining support groups, or becoming involved in social causes, we can find camaraderie and connection. Many people have found that sharing their stories of loss inspires others, creating a ripple effect that helps others heal, too. Community engagement gives us a sense of belonging and knowing that we are making a difference in others' lives can give new meaning to our own.

Finally, turning anger and grief into purpose helps us create a legacy that honors what we have endured and those we have loved. By channeling these emotions into positive action, we give our pain a voice that speaks not of despair, but of resilience.

This legacy can take many forms—advocating for change, creating art, mentoring others, or simply living in a way that reflects the values we hold dear. Each act, big or small, becomes a testament to the healing power of purpose. In time, what was once a source of suffering becomes a foundation for strength, and our stories become lights that guide others through their own struggles.

Ultimately, turning anger and grief into purpose is an ongoing journey. It does not erase the pain, but it reshapes it into something that contributes positively to our lives and the lives of others. In this way, we honor our own experiences and find new meaning in the face of hardship, knowing that even in the darkest moments, there is a way forward that brings healing, hope, and purpose.

Relationship Between Anger and Grief:

Understanding how grief often triggers feelings of anger, and how both emotions can coexist during the healing process.

Take time to discuss societal perceptions of these emotions, including stigmas and misconceptions that can hinder the healing process.

Find Meaning in Pain

Finding meaning in pain can be a transformative experience, turning what feels unbearable into a journey of growth and self-discovery.

Pain often reveals the depth of our values and connections, bringing into focus what we cherish most.

While it may not offer immediate comfort, pain teaches resilience and empathy, shaping our character in ways that joy alone could never achieve. When we embrace the lessons embedded in hardship, we can begin to see pain not as a roadblock but as a bridge to a deeper understanding of ourselves and the world.

Finding meaning in pain also allows us to connect with others in powerful ways, as shared suffering often forms the basis for genuine empathy. By acknowledging our struggles and allowing them to make us more compassionate, we turn personal hardship into a gift for others, offering support and solidarity. Pain can inspire us to help others heal, using our experiences as a source of strength and guidance.

Ultimately, finding meaning in pain does not erase the difficulty but transforms it, allowing us to live more fully, grounded in the knowledge that we have endured and can still contribute meaningfully to the lives of others.

Encouraging readers to set goals that resonate with their core values and passions, using their experiences as a compass for direction.

Staying Flexible and Open: Emphasizing the importance of flexibility in pursuing goals, allowing for adjustments as feelings evolve and circumstances change.

The Power of Small Actions: Highlighting that even small, intentional actions can lead to significant changes over time, reinforcing the idea that progress is a journey.

Sustaining Purpose and Growth

a. **Maintaining Momentum:** Strategies for sustaining motivation and commitment to goals, including regular reflection and reassessment of progress.
b. **Celebrating Achievements:** Understanding the importance of celebrating both small and large milestones in the journey toward purpose.
c. **Embracing the Process:** Recognizing that transformation is an ongoing journey, filled with ups and downs, and learning to embrace each step along the way.
d. **Creating a Legacy of Purpose:** How to envision the impact of transforming pain into purpose as a legacy that can inspire future generations, contributing to a cycle of healing and growth.

Takeaways and Reflections

a. **Harnessing Emotions as Catalysts for Change:** Recognizing that anger and grief, when processed healthily, can be powerful motivators for personal and societal change.
b. **Finding Strength in Vulnerability:** Embracing vulnerability as a pathway to discovering deeper connections and purpose in the aftermath of intense emotions.
c. **Empowerment Through Action:** Understanding that taking intentional steps toward meaningful goals can empower individuals to reclaim their narrative and foster resilience.

This chapter empowers you to embrace your anger and grief as vital components of your emotional journey.

By acknowledging and transforming these emotions into purposeful actions, you can foster healing, build resilience, and inspire others in their own journeys of transformation. Through this process, anger and grief can evolve from sources of pain into powerful catalysts for positive change and personal growth.

15.
MY HEALING PLACE No:121
(Finding solace and renewal)

*'Pain is a gift. It's meant to wake you up. It shows you
what you're supposed to heal and become.'*
Eckhart Tolle

This chapter, My Healing Place-121, I invite you to
explore the journey of seeking and creating spaces of
solace, comfort, and renewal amidst life's challenges.
Whether it's a physical location, a mental refuge, or a
community of support, the healing place represents the
environments, practices, and connections that foster deep
healing. In this chapter, you are guided to identify and
cultivate their own healing places, understand the role
these spaces play in mental and emotional recovery, and
integrate them into daily life as a source of ongoing
strength and peace.

The concept of a 'healing place' is deeply profound and
can vary significantly from one person to another,
influenced by personal experiences, relationships, and
environments.

Your reflections on your healing place, particularly at No. 121, highlight some key elements that are essential for true healing. Here's a more in-depth exploration of what happens at a healing place and why it's important to engage with the healing process:

My Healing Place: Definition and Significance

Physical Space

A healing place can be a physical location—a home, a community center, a serene environment—where individuals feel safe and supported.

At No. 121, for instance, the physical attributes of the space—its comfort, familiarity, and ambiance— contributes to a sense of belonging and security.

Emotional Support

The emotional landscape of a healing place is equally important. As I mentioned, the understanding and compassion of the leader, Ms. Tirzah, play a crucial role in fostering an environment conducive to healing. This implies that leaders and caregivers need to recognize and respect individual healing journeys, providing space for those in need to process their feelings without judgment or interruption.

Community Connection

At no 121, the community was and is very supportive and connected, examples of Mathew Hambuda, and leader of the place Ms Tirzah. Living with others who understand the healing process can create a network of empathy and shared experiences. To me this healing place became a sanctuary where myself and other individuals saw/see and heard, allowing for vulnerability without fear of rejection or misunderstanding.

The Process of Healing

 At 121 I saw people allowed or given to heal. And healing is not linear; it often involves navigating back to painful memories and feelings. This is what I found profound at 121, since it acknowledges this reality and allows individuals to confront their past at their own pace.

It's essential to understand that being in a healing place does not shield one from emotional pain or setbacks. Instead, it provides the support needed to process and move through those emotions.

The Role of Affection

At this place, those who had the grace to understand healing would give support to those who they thought needed it without bombarding with unnecessary questions but by simply showing affection to them. Simple acts of kindness, such as a hug or a shared moment of silence, can be incredibly powerful in a healing environment. These gestures can reaffirm a sense of safety and belonging, making it easier for individuals to lower their defenses and engage in the healing process. Sometimes, just being present with someone—without the need for words—can foster deep healing.

Plugging into Healing Virtues

Healing virtues—such as compassion, forgiveness, patience, and understanding—are essential in a healing place. To 'plug in' means to actively engage with these virtues, both within oneself and with others.

This Engagement Involves

a. **Reflection:** Taking time to understand one's emotions and responses to various situations.
b. **Acceptance:** Recognizing that healing takes time and that it's okay to feel hurt even in a supportive environment.
c. **Connection**: Building relationships with others in the space, fostering mutual understanding and support.

Ultimately, a healing place—whether physical or mental—serves as a sanctuary where individuals can explore their emotions, confront their past, and begin to heal. It is a space where patience and compassion are cultivated, allowing each person to find their unique path to recovery. While healing may not be guaranteed, the presence of understanding, love, and community can significantly enhance the process, making the journey toward healing more manageable and meaningful.

My observations about healing, especially in a communal environment like No. 121, reveal the complexities of personal growth and recovery. While the environment plays a significant role in the healing process, individual attitudes and choices can heavily influence outcomes. Here's a deeper exploration of why some individuals find healing while others do not, as well as the importance of soaking in healing virtues and developing life skills.

Duality of Healing Experiences

1. Individual Attitude and Openness

Healing is a deeply personal journey, and one of the most significant factors influencing whether someone heals is their mindset. An open and willing attitude towards healing—an acceptance of one's brokenness and a desire for change—can catalyze transformation. Conversely, individuals who resist confronting their pain or are cynical about the healing process may find themselves stuck, perceiving healing as unattainable.

a. **Defensive Mechanisms:** Some individuals may unconsciously build walls to protect themselves from further pain, making it difficult to accept the help offered in a healing place.

b. **Fear of Change:** Change can be intimidating; thus, the fear of what lies beyond their current pain can prevent some individuals from engaging in the healing process.

2. Personal Responsibility

Personal responsibility is a key factor in one's healing that's why I firmly believe that our healing requires our active participation. Those who embrace responsibility for their healing—acknowledging their role in both their pain and recovery—are more likely to experience positive outcomes. In contrast, individuals who blame external circumstances or others for their struggles may miss opportunities for growth.

Soaking in Healing Virtues- *(Important)*

Positive influences are important for one to immerse themselves in them. Soaking in healing virtues—qualities such as empathy, gratitude, and love—means actively engaging with and embodying these traits. This immersion can profoundly impact one's mindset and overall well-being.

Some Priceless Virtues here

a. **Compassion:** Learning to show compassion to oneself is crucial. It fosters self-acceptance and encourages individuals to treat themselves with kindness, making healing possible.
b. **Gratitude:** Cultivating a sense of gratitude, even for small victories in the healing process, can shift perspectives and promote resilience.

The reason why at 121 it is a conducive place for healing is mainly because it thrives on the collective energies of people around this place, a togetherness to embrace each other. When individuals engage with the healing virtues and support each other, the atmosphere becomes one of positivity and growth, enhancing everyone's chances of healing.

At 121, people share experiences as a way of encouraging each other. Not a trivia practice but very important to hear success stories from pain. Sharing stories of struggle and resilience can inspire others, creating a ripple effect of healing within the community.

Life Skills as a Component of Healing

Learning and Growth: The transition from pain to healing often involves developing life skills that can contribute to self-sufficiency and personal empowerment. As individuals heal, they often seek to acquire skills that can help them lead productive lives.

Ma Tirzah, always says to habitants at 121, she is proud to see people growing their skills and improving their lives.

Income-Generating Projects: Engaging in skills training or income-generating projects not only provides practical benefits but also enhances self-esteem and fosters a sense of purpose. Successfully learning a skill can solidify the belief that healing is achievable. At 121, those who find and horn their skills, live fruitfully and those who don't really grow their skills end up being frustrated by almost everything and pick up petty fights. While you are at your healing place and healing, it is time to identify skills and put them to use, they contribute to your healing journey.

The Toxicity of Unhealed Individuals: An unhealed person can inadvertently become toxic to themselves and those around them. Pain that is not addressed often manifests as negativity, resentment, and emotional volatility, which can strain relationships and diminish overall community well-being.an unhealed person picks up fights with everyone and still blame others than their state of broken, hurting and not healed.

Cycle of Hurt: When individuals who have not processed their pain interact with others, they may project their unresolved issues onto those around them, perpetuating a cycle of hurt. I have seen individuals in life and at 121, who are stuck in the cycle of hurt.

The journey of healing is multi-faceted, requiring a combination of individual willingness, community support, and the cultivation of healing virtues. While the environment at No. 121 provides the necessary ingredients for recovery, the ultimate outcome rests on individual attitudes and choices.

To embrace healing, one must actively soak in positive influences and virtues, recognize the importance of personal responsibility, and take steps toward acquiring life skills that promote independence and confidence. Healing is indeed a process that requires effort, and it's through this effort that individuals can transform their lives and, in turn, uplift those around them. This shared experience of growth and learning not only benefits individuals but can foster a thriving, supportive community that continues to heal and inspire.

Concept of a Healing Place

Defining the healing place as any sanctuary—physical or emotional—that allows for rest, reflection, and renewal. At 121 there is place called the **'Upper-room'**, known as a place for solitudes and prayerful conversations. Whereby one pours their soul on the altar for healings and restoration.

Exploring how healing places differ for each individual, whether a literal space, like a room or natural setting, or an emotional sanctuary found in relationships or practices.

Understanding the healing place as essential for processing pain, reconnecting with inner peace, and revitalizing one's spirit.

Power of Physical Healing Spaces

a. Based on observations and experiences, I have seen at 121, how physical locations—gardens, rooms, places of worship, or natural landscapes—can create an atmosphere of safety, calm, and healing.

b. There should be guidance for all on creating a personal healing space at home or finding accessible locations that evoke calmness and inner peace.

Emotional Healing Spaces and Mental Safe Havens

a. We do this by creating mental healing places through visualization, meditation, and mindfulness practices.

b. Developing the techniques to construct a mental 'sanctuary' where one can retreat when feeling overwhelmed or distressed.

We learn to use these mental spaces to navigate challenging emotions, re-center, and find a sense of grounding.

Supportive Communities its role

Recognizing the importance of supportive relationships and communities as vital healing places, from family and friends to support groups and faith communities.

How genuine connection with others fosters healing through shared experiences, understanding, and encouragement.

Cultivating these relationships and being mindful of finding communities that nourish rather than drain one's energy.

We Heal through Rituals and Practices

a. One must learn to do journaling, prayer, or creative arts—
that can act as healing places through consistent, reflective
engagement.

b. By engaging in these and other rituals can provide
stability, offer us comfort, and encourage self-reflection,
becoming a personal refuge of sorts.

c. One must discover and regularly engage in their chosen
practices as a means of self-care and growth.

Know your Healing Places

a. As for me 121 is my healing place, your healing place is
your refreshing and refuelling place .one must understand
how regular visits to one's healing places—physical,
mental, or social— help build resilience and strength to
face future challenges. It can also be termed you Grace
Place, your healing place.

b. One should be encouraged to develop strategies to draw
on the peace and strength from healing places in times of
stress or crisis.

I firmly encourage you to treat your healing place as a vital
resource, revisiting and nurturing it regularly to maintain
well-being.

Bring your Healing Place into your Everyday

a. Here are some practical tips for you and me to make
healing an ongoing, integrated part of daily life rather than
a retreat during crises alone.

b. Here I emphasize the importance of small daily rituals and reminders that connect you with healing place and provide consistent grounding.

c. My role is to make you see your healing as a lifelong journey and the healing place as a reliable source of comfort and renewal throughout life's ups and downs.

Takeaways and Reflections

a. **Healing is a Sanctuary:** Identify and nurture spaces, both physical and mental, that offer calm, safety, and support during times of hardship.

b. **Regularly Revisit the Healing Place:** Make time for these sanctuaries regularly to build resilience and maintain emotional and mental health, not just in times of distress but as part of everyday life.

c. **Connect to Nature and Community:** Recognize the power of nature and community as timeless healing spaces that foster deep growth, acceptance, and perspective.

In this chapter I offer you insights and practical guidance on creating and maintaining your healing places, encouraging you to find and nurture your spaces of solace for resilience, balance, and personal growth.

This chapter emphasizes that healing is not only a response to pain but also a proactive part of sustaining inner peace and well-being.

16.
BRUISED AND BATTERED BUT HEALED

'*In the depth of winter, I finally learned that within me there lay an invincible summer.*'
Albert Camus

In Bruised and Battered but Healed, I explore with you the profound journey of recovery that follows trauma, loss, or deep emotional pain. In this deep chapter we acknowledge the scars left behind by painful experiences while emphasizing the resilience of the human spirit and the potential for healing. Through stories of triumph, practical healing strategies, and insights into the recovery process, you will learn how to embrace your scars as symbols of strength rather than weakness. This chapter serves as a reminder that while we may be bruised and battered, healing is not only possible but also transformative.

In Bruised and Battered but Healed, the exploration of recovery after trauma serves as both a testament to the human spirit and a beacon of hope for those who have faced their own struggles. The journey through emotional pain and loss can leave deep scars, but these marks do not define us; rather, they narrate a story of resilience, strength, and the transformative power of healing.

Scars are Marks of Survival

Understanding Scars as Reminders: Scars symbolize the experiences we have endured, each one a physical or emotional reminder of battles fought.

They tell stories of courage, vulnerability, and survival. In acknowledging our scars, we honor the journey we have travelled—recognizing both the pain we have faced and the lessons we have learned.

a. **Narratives of Strength:** Each scar carries a narrative. They remind us of moments when we stood firm in the face of adversity, illustrating our capacity to endure and grow.

b. **Scars are our Tutors:** Every scar represents a lesson learned through hardship. These experiences can shape our perspectives, deepen our empathy, and inform our choices moving forward. Embracing our scars encourages a mindset that views challenges as opportunities for growth, rather than mere reminders of suffering.

c. **Lessons in Resilience:** The journey of healing fosters resilience. With each painful experience, we learn coping strategies, discover our inner strength, and build a toolkit for navigating future challenges.

Resilience of the Human Spirit

In the face of life's greatest hardships, the human spirit has an incredible capacity to endure and adapt. Pain, though often viewed as a burden, becomes a powerful teacher, reshaping our understanding of strength and purpose. Every struggle reveals hidden reservoirs of courage, transforming ordinary people into remarkable survivors.

This resilience is not merely about overcoming difficulties but embracing them as essential steps on the journey to growth. Through pain, we learn that our limitations are often illusions, and that every trial we face makes us more than we were before.

Taught and Schooled by Pain illuminates this journey, showing how resilience emerges as a quiet, steadfast force within. It is in our darkest hours that we discover grace— an unyielding presence that guides us through, urging us to rise when all seems lost. Pain refines us, teaching us compassion, wisdom, and the value of perseverance. As we navigate our struggles, we come to understand that resilience is not just survival; it is the determination to thrive. In the end, we find that pain has been a companion, pushing us towards a life we never thought possible.

The Journey Toward Healing: Recovery from trauma is often a winding path, filled with ups and downs. The acknowledgment of scars is just one step in a broader healing process. As we navigate this journey, we must allow ourselves the grace to feel pain while also striving toward healing.

Embracing Vulnerability: True healing requires vulnerability. It is in facing our pain, rather than shying away from it, that we can begin to transform our scars into symbols of strength.

Moving Beyond Fear: When we fully heal, our scars are not something to fear or hide.

They become part of our story—a testament to the battles we have faced and the victories we have achieved. This shift in perspective empowers us to live authentically, embracing both our flaws and our triumphs.

From Shame to Pride: The process of healing allows us to transform any shame associated with our scars into pride. Instead of viewing our scars as blemishes, we can see them as badges of honor that reflect our journeys and the lessons learned along the way.

The Power of Community and Support

Sharing Our Stories: Sharing the stories behind our scars can foster connection and understanding within our communities. When we open up about our struggles, we not only liberate ourselves from the weight of isolation but also inspire others to embrace their own healing journeys.

Building Empathy: Through storytelling, we can build bridges of empathy, creating safe spaces for others to share their experiences and find support. This communal healing reinforces the idea that we are not alone in our battles.

Celebrating Healing: As we move toward healing, it is essential to celebrate our progress, no matter how small. Each step taken, each scar acknowledged, and each lesson learned deserves recognition. Celebrating these milestones fosters a sense of accomplishment and reinforces our commitment to growth.

Creating a Culture of Healing: By celebrating healing, we cultivate a culture that embraces vulnerability and resilience, encouraging others to embark on their own journeys of recovery.

In Bruised and Battered but Healed, the narrative unfolds as a powerful reminder that scars are not signs of defeat, but rather evidence of survival and growth. They indicate that we have faced challenges and emerged on the other side, carrying valuable lessons and a renewed understanding of ourselves.

By embracing our scars as symbols of resilience, we can inspire others to view their own journeys through a lens of hope and strength. Healing is not about erasing the past, but about acknowledging it, learning from it, and allowing it to shape us into the individuals we are meant to be. Ultimately, the journey of healing transforms our scars from reminders of pain into symbols of triumph, illuminating the incredible resilience of the human spirit.

Acknowledging the Bruises

Acknowledging the bruises means recognizing the emotional, mental, and physical scars we carry from life's battles. These bruises are not signs of weakness but symbols of survival and strength. Every mark tells a story of endurance, a testament to the resilience that has carried us through. When we face our bruises openly, we allow ourselves the healing and growth that comes from acceptance.

Embracing these imperfections is a key step in transforming pain into power and realizing that it's not the wounds that define us, but how we rise from them.

The Journey of Healing

The journey of healing is not linear, nor is it one-size-fits-all; it's a deeply personal process that requires patience, introspection, and resilience. For many, including myself, Herbert, it begins with the painful realization that healing must take place—it is the acknowledgement of brokenness, whether it's emotional, mental, or physical. Healing demands vulnerability, as we must confront our past and the wounds that have shaped us, not hiding from them but allowing them the space to be seen and felt. It is a journey of gradual transformation, where we learn to forgive, accept, and release the weight of pain that once held us down.

Along the way, there are moments of doubt and setbacks, but the key to healing is perseverance. We discover that healing is not about forgetting the pain but learning to live with it, finding meaning and purpose in our scars. As we walk this path, we uncover new strengths, deeper wisdom, and a sense of peace we once thought impossible. Through this process, we realize that healing is not just about the absence of pain, but the ability to move forward with hope and an open heart.

Just as I have walked this path, others too can find the courage to embrace their own journey of healing, knowing that it's never too late to begin.

Transforming Pain into Purpose

Transforming pain into purpose is the powerful act of finding meaning and direction in our struggles. Pain often feels like a burden, a force that diminishes us, but when we shift our perspective, it can become the catalyst for growth and transformation. It teaches us valuable lessons about resilience, empathy, and our own strength. By embracing our pain, we allow it to guide us toward a greater understanding of ourselves and the world around us.

As we turn our pain into purpose, we not only heal but also inspire others, showing that even in our darkest moments, there is potential for light and impact.

Celebrating Healing and Progress

Celebrating healing and progress is about acknowledging the milestones in our journey, no matter how small they may seem. It's recognizing that healing is not an instant transformation, but a gradual process that unfolds with time, effort, and patience. Each step forward, whether it's a day without pain, a moment of clarity, or a breakthrough in understanding, deserves to be celebrated. Progress is often measured not by perfection but by the courage to continue moving forward despite the setbacks.

Celebrating these victories serves as a reminder that healing is possible, that we have grown stronger, and that we are worthy of joy, even after enduring pain.

It's a moment to honor how far we've come and to encourage ourselves and others to keep moving toward the fullness of life that lies ahead.

Moving Forward with Strength

Moving forward with strength means embracing the resilience within us and using it to overcome the challenges that still lie ahead. It's about acknowledging the pain we've endured without allowing it to define or limit us. Strength comes from the lessons we learn along the way—the wisdom gained through hardships, the courage to face uncertainty, and the determination to keep going, even when the road is tough.

Moving forward is not about forgetting the past, but about using it as a foundation to build a stronger, more determined version of ourselves. Each step forward, no matter how difficult, reinforces our capacity to face future struggles with even greater resolve, knowing that the strength we've cultivated will carry us through any storm.

Takeaways and Reflections

Embracing Scars as Symbols of Strength: Recognizing that the bruises and scars from our past can serve as powerful reminders of our resilience and capacity to heal.

The Transformative Power of Healing: Understanding that healing is not just about recovery but also about personal transformation and the discovery of new strengths and purposes.

Living Beyond Pain: Empowering readers to embrace their journey beyond pain, cultivating a life that reflects their growth, resilience, and renewed sense of self.

The scars we carry on our bodies and in our hearts tell stories far deeper than words alone. Each scar is a testament to survival, resilience, and the divine grace that has seen us through life's most challenging moments. For you, these physical scars—especially the one across your stomach from the accident in Zambia—are powerful reminders of battles fought, both won and lost, and the unmatched strength that has carried you forward.

Scars as Symbols of Survival

1. Marks of Life's Trials: The scars etched on your body are not mere blemishes but symbols of the trials you've endured. They speak of moments where life tested your strength, pushing you to your limits, yet you survived. Each scar holds a chapter of your story—a narrative of resilience in the face of adversity. They are markers of the physical and emotional wounds you've encountered along the way, and proof that you've emerged from them, still standing.

A Testament to Endurance: Scars represent the battles of life—some of which were fierce, painful, and unforgettable. Yet, by bearing these scars, you embody a spirit that refuses to be defeated.

2. The Stomach Scar: Surviving the Unthinkable The scar on your stomach, a result of a traumatic accident in Zambia, is especially significant. It's a stark reminder of the fragility of life, of the moments when survival was uncertain. The memory of that accident and the wreckage left behind brings an acute awareness of the miraculousness of life. The bus was reduced to ashes, yet you were saved, a reminder of divine intervention and the grace that spared you.

Survival Amidst Loss: Walking away from that accident with your life, even though others may not have been as fortunate, speaks to the mystery and grace that surrounds us. This scar, in particular, symbolizes both pain and gratitude for the chance to continue your journey.

Seeing God's Hand in the Scars

a. **Divine Grace and Unmatched Love** As you look upon your scars, you see God's hand in each one—a< reminder of His presence during your darkest moments. Each mark speaks to the unmatchable love and protection that have guided you through life's storms. The scar on your stomach and others on your body are physical manifestations of the times you were held, protected, and given a second chance to continue your journey.

b. **A Reminder of Divine Purpose:** Surviving such intense battles can feel overwhelming, but the scars left behind reassure you of a purpose still to be fulfilled.
Your scars remind you that your life has value and meaning, and that there is a reason for your survival.

c. **Gracefully Still Standing:** To look at your scars and acknowledge God's love is to embrace a truth many people struggle with—that the pain we endure can be transformative. These scars are not signs of weakness but of a fierce, graceful strength. They remind you that, no matter what challenges arise, you have been given the resilience to overcome them.

d. **Gratitude in Survival:** When you reflect on the battles you've survived, the sense of gratitude deepens. Each scar becomes a point of reflection on how far you've come, an opportunity to honor the journey you've travelled.
Scars as Sources of Strength

Scars are not just remnants of past pain; they are powerful symbols of resilience and survival.

Each scar tells a unique story of struggle, endurance, and healing. While they may remind us of our wounds, they also reflect our ability to overcome adversity and emerge stronger. Far from signs of weakness, scars represent the strength it took to endure and the growth that followed. They serve as constant reminders that, despite the pain we've faced, we have the inner fortitude to continue moving forward. Embracing our scars allows us to transform them into sources of strength, showing the world that we are not defined by our injuries, but by the courage and wisdom we've gained from them.

Giving Back: Sharing your journey, including the scars, is a way of passing on the strength you've gained. You offer a beacon of hope to others, showing them that scars are not the end of the story but part of a journey that can lead to healing and growth.

Your scars are powerful reminders of survival, endurance, and divine grace. Each one is a physical reflection of the resilience within you, and they represent both the pain and the blessings of life's journey. By recognizing God's hand in your scars, you honor the battles you've faced and the strength that has carried you through.

These scars are not just marks; they are symbols of a life lived with courage and faith. Embracing them with gratitude allows you to see each challenge as a step in a larger journey, where you continue to stand, gracefully resilient, with the purpose and strength to inspire others along the way.

This chapter encourages you and me to honor our experiences of being bruised and battered while celebrating our capacity to heal and transform.

By recognizing the strength gained from adversity, you and me can move forward with hope, purpose, and a profound understanding of their resilience. In embracing both our scars and our healing, we discover a deeper sense of self and the potential for a fulfilling life beyond pain.

17.
ONLY SCARS REMAIN
(But I am healed)

'Out of suffering have emerged the strongest souls; the most massive characters are seared with scars.'
Khalil Gibran

In life, pain often feels like a force that defines us, but over time, it becomes a teacher. The emotional, physical, or mental wounds we carry can leave marks—scars—that never truly fade. However, these scars are not a reflection of who we are but a testament to the battles we've fought and the resilience we've shown. Scars are the only visible remnants of the pain we've endured, but they also tell a deeper story of healing and transformation. They remind us of the strength it took to rise, the lessons we learned, and the courage we found to move forward.

In this chapter, I want to explore the delicate balance between the pain that shapes us and the healing that leads us to a place of peace. This chapter serves as a powerful affirmation that healing does not mean forgetting but rather integrating experiences into a new narrative of hope and empowerment.

The journey toward healing begins with acknowledgment. For many of us, including myself, there was a time when pain felt all-consuming. Whether it was personal struggles, setbacks in life, or deep emotional wounds, the weight seemed unbearable.

Yet, through the process of healing, we learn to understand that pain is not a permanent state. It's a passage—an experience that, while painful, serves to teach us something valuable about ourselves. We often don't realize it in the moment, but as time passes, the pain begins to loosen its grip, and we start to see the world with a new perspective.

This transformation isn't instantaneous, but it's powerful. Healing, much like growth, is slow and subtle, but once we look back, we realize how far we've come.

The scars we carry may be reminders of pain, but they are also symbols of survival. When I reflect on my own journey, I recognize that my scars are part of what has shaped me into who I am today. They are not imperfections but marks of progress. They signify that I endured and emerged stronger. For example, many people who knew me growing up thought I would never amount to much. I was quiet, withdrawn, and came from a humble background. Yet, through the trials I faced, I learned to embrace my scars—not with shame, but with pride. They are proof that I have overcome the obstacles that once threatened to hold me back.

As the scars remain, we are often left to reconcile with them. It's natural to feel a sense of loss or sadness when we reflect on the pain we've experienced, but it's essential to understand that healing does not mean forgetting.

Healing means making peace with what happened, accepting that it was part of our story, and choosing to move forward.

Our scars are not something to hide but something to honor. They are reminders of the strength we've built, the lessons we've learned, and the resilience we possess. Healing is not the absence of pain, but the ability to move beyond it and find new meaning in the experience.

In this chapter, we explore the notion that pain has a purpose. Pain teaches us empathy, resilience, and the depth of our own capacity for growth. It's through our struggles that we find our true strength. Just as a diamond is formed under pressure, we too are shaped by the challenges we face. Our scars become part of our story, making us who we are—a story of perseverance, transformation, and ultimately, healing.

Through every trial, I learned that healing is not a destination but a journey—a journey of discovering our worth, acknowledging our scars, and realizing that while pain may have shaped us, it does not define us. The scars remain as reminders of how far we've come, but the healing is what allows us to live fully, embracing life with newfound strength and hope.

As I continue to move forward, I carry my scars with me—not as burdens, but as sources of strength. The only thing that remains from the pain is the scar, but the healing is within me. Every day,

I become more and more aware of how far I've come and how much strength I now carry in my spirit. Healing doesn't mean the absence of pain—it means finding peace within it, growing through it, and discovering the person you were always meant to be.

Understanding Scars as Symbols

The Stories Behind Scars: Sharing personal stories of individuals who have turned their scars into powerful narratives of resilience and healing.

Takeaways and Reflections

a. **Scars as Testaments of Resilience:** Understanding that scars symbolize not just the pain endured but also the strength and resilience developed through the healing process.
b. **Embracing a Transformed Identity**: Recognizing that healing leads to personal transformation and a deeper understanding of oneself, where scars become a part of one's unique story.
c. **Living Beyond Pain:** Empowering readers to embrace their lives beyond pain, using their experiences and scars as catalysts for growth, connection, and purpose.

This chapter serves as an empowering conclusion to the healing journey, reminding you and me that while scars may remain, they are signs of survival, resilience, and profound personal growth.

By embracing your scars, you can forge a new path forward—one defined by hope, strength, and the courage to live fully despite the pain of the past. In recognizing that healing is an ongoing journey, you are encouraged to continue embracing life with an open heart and mind, celebrating the beauty of your scars along the way.

18.
EMOTIONAL HEALING
KEY TO BRINGING PEACE IN ONE'S LIFE

'The wound is the place where the light enters you.'
Rumi

In the journey toward inner peace, emotional healing stands as a crucial steppingstone. The process of healing emotional wounds is essential not only for achieving stability but also for cultivating a deep, lasting peace. Just as physical injuries require attention and care to mend, so too do the emotional hurts and traumas that accumulate over time. When unaddressed, these emotional wounds can become barriers to personal growth, healthy relationships, and genuine happiness.

However, through emotional healing, we can restore inner harmony and move forward with renewed purpose.

Emotional healing is the process of reclaiming our inner peace and well-being after experiencing emotional pain or trauma. Often, emotional pain can stem from past relationships, loss, unmet expectations, or even unhealed wounds from childhood. While these experiences can leave us feeling broken, they do not have to define us. Healing begins when we acknowledge the hurt, we feel and choose to confront it, rather than allowing it to fester in the background of our lives.

The first step is recognizing that emotional healing is not linear; there will be good days and bad, but with each step, we move closer to a place of peace. It requires patience, self-compassion, and the courage to heal.

One of the critical aspects of emotional healing is self-awareness. Understanding the emotions you are dealing with is crucial for managing them. Many people spend years suppressing their emotions because they feel that acknowledging them will make them vulnerable. However, repressing emotions only creates more turmoil within. Emotional healing begins when we give ourselves permission to feel—whether it's sadness, anger, or fear. When we allow ourselves to sit with these emotions, we start to understand them better, and in turn, we gain control over them. This self-awareness allows us to make conscious decisions to move toward healing, rather than remaining stuck in emotional patterns that no longer serve us.

Forgiveness plays a significant role in emotional healing. Holding onto grudges or resentment creates emotional weight, blocking us from experiencing peace. Forgiveness doesn't mean condoning hurtful actions; rather, it means releasing the emotional grip that these actions have on us.

When we forgive, we free ourselves from the pain of the past and open the door to emotional liberation. This is not always an easy process, and it may take time, but it's necessary for healing. Forgiving others and ourselves allows us to let go of the negative emotions that bind us, making room for healing and peace to enter our hearts.

Another important component of emotional healing is self-compassion. When we are dealing with emotional pain, it's easy to become self-critical, blaming ourselves for what happened or for not being able to 'fix' our emotions quickly. But healing cannot happen in an atmosphere of self-judgment. We must learn to be gentle with ourselves and treat ourselves with the same kindness we would offer to a friend. This means accepting that healing takes time and that there is no shame in struggling. Self-compassion involves being patient and loving with ourselves as we work through our emotions, rather than rushing the process or beating ourselves up for not being 'healed' yet. When we practice self-compassion, we foster a safe internal environment in which emotional healing can take root.

Building resilience is another key aspect of emotional healing. Resilience is the ability to bounce back from adversity, to find strength in times of difficulty. When we heal emotionally, we become more resilient because we learn from our challenges and become better equipped to handle future difficulties. Resilience is not about avoiding pain, but about facing it head-on and emerging stronger. It's through emotional healing that we learn that we are far more capable of coping with life's challenges than we originally believed. The journey of emotional healing transforms us, teaching us how to respond to life's hardships with grace, wisdom, and strength.

The healing process also involves letting go of past hurts and embracing the present. Holding onto past emotional wounds can keep us stuck in a cycle of pain, preventing us from fully enjoying the life we have now.

This doesn't mean forgetting or ignoring the past, but rather learning to release its power over our present and future. Healing requires a shift in mindset—moving from a place of victimhood to one of empowerment. We cannot change what has happened, but we can change how we respond to it. By letting go of the emotional baggage of the past, we create space for joy, peace, and fulfillment in our lives.

Emotional healing is the key to unlocking peace in our lives. It is a process that requires us to confront our pain, embrace our emotions, and practice forgiveness and self-compassion. While it may be challenging at times, the journey toward healing is incredibly rewarding. As we heal, we become more resilient, more aware of our inner strength, and more capable of navigating life's ups and downs with peace. By letting go of the emotional wounds that have weighed us down, we make room for happiness, balance, and inner harmony.

Emotional healing is not about erasing the past, but about transforming it into a source of growth and wisdom. In the end, peace comes not from avoiding emotional pain but from learning how to heal it and move forward with grace.

19.
THE LESSONS OF LOSS

'Sometimes, you have to learn a lesson through pain.
Sometimes, it's the only way to teach us.'
Unknown

Loss is one of life's most profound teachers. When we lose something or someone dear to us, we are often left to confront a void that feels insurmountable. In the depths of grief, we face a type of pain that permeates every aspect of our being, reshaping the way we see ourselves, our relationships, and our place in the world. Yet, while loss is undeniably painful, it also carries within it the potential to transform us in ways we may never have anticipated.

The Depth of Grief

Grief is complex and multifaceted; it is not merely an emotional response but a journey that encompasses everything from disbelief and anger to acceptance and adaptation. In the throes of loss, we often encounter our own vulnerability and the temporary nature of life.

This awareness, though unsettling, encourages us to look beyond the superficial and reassess what truly matters. As we navigate grief, we find that it calls us to slow down, to reflect, and to gain a deeper understanding of our values and priorities.

Redefining Priorities

One of the most significant lessons of loss is the clarity it brings to our priorities.

When we experience the absence of someone or something deeply valued, we begin to see what is most important in life. Grief often strips away our attachments to trivial pursuits, redirecting our focus toward meaningful relationships, personal growth, and experiences that bring genuine joy. In learning what we are willing to let go of, we simultaneously learn what we are determined to hold close.

This redefinition of priorities is not only a coping mechanism but a transformative shift in perspective. As we grapple with loss, we often come to recognize that much of what we previously deemed essential holds little weight compared to the people we love and the moments we cherish. This newfound clarity guides us toward a life of greater intention, one rooted in authenticity and aligned with our most heartfelt values.

Deepening Empathy and Compassion

The experience of loss connects us to others in ways we may not have previously understood. In our own grief, we develop a profound empathy for the suffering of others, recognizing the shared human experience of loss. This deepened sense of compassion opens us up to being more present, patient, and understanding with those around us.

We begin to see that each person carries their own struggles, and this realization fosters a stronger sense of connection and community.

Grief transforms us into more compassionate people, capable of showing kindness and understanding to those in pain. This shift not only heals our own wounds but serves as a foundation for supporting others, allowing us to be present in a way that goes beyond words. Through the lessons of loss, we learn to offer comfort, knowing the power of a listening ear or a silent presence.

Embracing Impermanence

Loss teaches us the impermanence of all things. It brings to light the transient nature of life and forces us to come to terms with the fact that nothing is guaranteed. This realization, though difficult to accept, can lead to a more profound appreciation for each moment. When we embrace the fleeting nature of life, we learn to live with greater awareness and gratitude, cherishing each experience as it comes and savoring the presence of those, we hold dear.

This acceptance of impermanence encourages us to live fully, to be more present, and to invest our energy in what genuinely fulfills us. While the pain of loss remains, it also becomes a motivator—a reminder to make the most of the time we have and to pursue a life of purpose and connection.

Finding Meaning in Loss

Though loss can leave us feeling empty, many find that over time, it offers an opportunity for self-discovery and growth. By reflecting on the impact of what or who we have lost, we may uncover insights into our own beliefs, values, and strengths.

This process, often known as 'meaning making', helps us to integrate the experience of loss into our lives in a way that fosters resilience and understanding.

Finding meaning in loss does not diminish the pain, but it provides a pathway to healing. For some, this may mean carrying on the legacy of a loved one, making life choices that honor their memory, or cultivating qualities they embodied. For others, it may mean using their experience to help others navigate similar paths. In these ways, loss becomes not an end, but a part of our journey that enriches our sense of purpose and strengthens our resolve.

The Gift of Transformation

While loss may leave permanent scars, it also has the power to transform us, revealing depths of resilience, courage, and wisdom that we may not have known were within us. As we learn to live with loss, we emerge with a heightened appreciation for life's fragility and beauty, more open to love, connection, and gratitude. The experience of loss, though painful, becomes a profound catalyst for growth, guiding us toward a life of deeper fulfillment and more authentic connection.

In the end, the lessons of loss teach us not only about what we have lost but about what remains—and what truly matters. These lessons encourage us to live with greater clarity, purpose, and compassion, allowing us to move forward with a renewed sense of what is most meaningful in life. Grief may change us, but in that change lies the potential for a life that is richer, more intentional, and more deeply felt.

May we carry forward the wisdom gained from our losses, honoring them as steppingstones on the path to a life of resilience, love, and understanding.

20.
THE UNTOLD MYSTERY OF SUICIDE

Suicide is often veiled in silence, stigma, and deep misunderstanding. Many struggle to comprehend what drives someone to the edge, and in the aftermath, those left behind are haunted by questions that may never be answered. As much as we try to unpack its causes and recognize the warning signs, suicide remains, in many ways, an untold mystery—an enigma woven into personal pain, hidden struggles, and sometimes years of unacknowledged mental and emotional strain.

In this chapter, I explore with you real stories that reveal the complexity of suicide, where external pressures, internal battles, and silent suffering converged into irreversible tragedy. These stories highlight the need for empathy, open dialogue, and understanding to help prevent others from slipping silently into despair. Take note the names of the people mentioned here in this chapter and book, except mine and family members have been changed to protect the people, but these are all written with full permission of the people.

Themba was a successful businessman, well-regarded in his community and loved by family and friends. On the surface, he appeared confident and resilient, always the life of the party and willing to lend a helping hand. However, what people didn't see was the intense pressure he felt to live up to these expectations.

 Privately, Themba battled chronic depression, a struggle he concealed even from those closest to him.

When his business faced a major financial setback, Themba became increasingly isolated. His friends noticed his absence at gatherings, but his well-known "strong" personality made them believe he would bounce back. In the final weeks, he withdrew even more, and when he died by suicide, the shock left his family and friends grappling with guilt and confusion. His story is a reminder of how outward appearances can hide profound internal pain, and how vital it is to reach out, even to those who seem the strongest.

Nothando's life changed forever when she lost her daughter in a tragic accident. The grief was devastating, and though her family and community offered support, the emptiness Nothando felt was unimaginable. She carried a profound sense of guilt, wondering if there was something she could have done differently. Rather than sharing her sorrow with others, Nothando retreated into silence, feeling that her pain was a burden to those around her.
Over time, her family noticed subtle changes—she became quieter, and her joy seemed to vanish. Her husband and children attempted to console her, but her grief was so deep and her silence so profound that she began to feel hopeless. Nothando's story illustrates how grief, when unexpressed, can weigh so heavily on the heart that it seems there is no escape.

Her family's enduring love was not enough to penetrate the wall of isolation that grief had built, and tragically, she took her own life.

This story underscores the need for open channels of communication, particularly in the face of loss, and highlights how, in times of profound sorrow, people need to know they are not alone, even if they can't fully express their pain.

Bongani was only sixteen, a quiet teenager with a passion for art and dreams of becoming a graphic designer. But Bongani's life at school was far from the hopeful world he imagined; he faced relentless bullying. His peers mocked him, targeted him on social media, and humiliated him publicly. Despite his pain, Bongani hid his suffering, putting on a brave face at home and pretending to be fine. Inside, though, he was desperate, struggling to find any escape from the daily torment he endured.

One day, after an especially cruel incident, Bongani left a note saying he couldn't bear the pain anymore. His family was devastated, unaware of the torment he had been facing. Bongani's tragic story reminds us of the harsh impact of bullying and the necessity of creating safe environments where young people can talk about their struggles. In his memory, his family started an anti-bullying campaign, hoping to prevent others from experiencing the same pain he endured in silence.

My brother Shepherd was a quiet, solitary man whose life was marked by challenges that seemed to shape and redefine him over the years.

His journey through two marriages, each fraught with its own struggles, mirrored a life touched by unresolved pain. His first marriage was also his first relationship, a commitment he made directly out of high school, and unfortunately, he was abused also in this marriage. Shepherd's schooling had ended abruptly after he was expelled for a student strike, an event that weighed heavily on him. As the head boy, he was held accountable for the strike, and I suspect he never fully recovered from that moment of blame and exclusion.

Shepherd had always been one to avoid confrontation, preferring peace to conflict—a nature that sometimes made him the first to step in to protect others, even acting as a shield for my other brothers when they were bullied. In his second marriage, he faced new challenges; disagreements arose between him and his wife about where to settle after he resigned from his job. This issue of relocation created a rift between them, and despite his quiet nature, the disagreement weighed heavily on him. In a tragic turn, he took his own life just days after leaving home. His story speaks to the silent burdens he carried and the unresolved struggles he endured, a reminder of the importance of understanding and support, even for those who seem at peace on the outside.

Suicide victims live a life of perfectionism in their minds that many a times costs them their lives, everything according to them must be perfect and right.

These stories reveal a powerful truth: unspoken struggles and unseen pain can have devastating consequences. Society often reinforces the need to 'keep up appearances' encouraging people to hide their pain and maintain a façade. Yet it is precisely this pressure to appear perfect that can isolate individuals, convincing them that they have to endure their struggles alone.

In some cultures, discussing mental health or personal challenges is seen as taboo, and people are urged to "be strong" or keep their problems to themselves. In my Zulu culture it is said loud and clear, 'A man doesn't cry', this has cost us lives of many men and seems to be now embedded in the lives and minds of many men world-wide.

The stigma around mental health issues creates further barriers, preventing people from reaching out for the help they so desperately need. Many people who die by suicide have endured years of hidden struggle—an untold mystery that only deepens after their passing. In understanding these tragic stories, we must commit ourselves to creating a world where vulnerability is met with compassion, where mental health conversations are normalized, and where individuals feel safe to share their inner battles.

Every life lost to suicide is a powerful reminder that silence can be deadly. To unravel the mystery of suicide, we must foster a culture that prioritizes listening, empathy, and open dialogue.

Rather than waiting for signs of visible distress, we can regularly check in with those we care about, encouraging honest conversations without judgment or stigma.

Support systems—be they family, friends, counsellors, or community groups—play a crucial role in helping individuals process life's hardships. By offering safe spaces for people to share their experiences and speak freely, we can help those carrying hidden pain find relief, knowing they are seen, valued, and not alone.

The journey to address this hidden pain requires a shift in were reaching out for help is seen not as a weakness but as a strength. By breaking the silence surrounding suicide, we honor those who have been lost to hidden suffering and make strides toward a future where fewer lives are lost to the shadows of unexpressed pain.

The stories of Themba, Nothando, Bongani, my brother and countless others show the urgent need to address the untold mysteries behind suicide. Hidden struggles and silent suffering have the power to erode even the strongest spirits. Through empathy, awareness, and a commitment to open dialogue, we can create a culture that acknowledges pain, supports healing, and, ultimately, saves lives.
In sharing these stories, we gain insight into the minds and hearts of those who may be struggling and learn the importance of stepping in before it's too late.

Each life is precious, and every story is a testament to the resilience and hope we can foster when we choose to listen, care, and support each other. Let us use these narratives not only as reminders of the fragility of the human spirit but as motivation to build a world that nurtures, protects, and values every individual.

21.
SUICIDE FEEDS
(On unexpressed and unacknowledged pain)

I will write and say this again and again that pain is a universal experience—whether from loss, disappointment, or heartbreak, every individual encounters it. However, not all pain is dealt with openly or even acknowledged. Many people, driven by fear, pride, or a sense of shame, choose to bury their suffering. But unexpressed and unacknowledged pain doesn't fade away with time; it intensifies. This hidden anguish can fester into feelings of hopelessness, and when left unchecked, it sometimes leads individuals to a place where they believe that escape is the only option.

In the shadows of unspoken sorrow, where voices are silenced by fear or self-doubt, suicide often finds its strongest footing. It is here, in this dark terrain of silent suffering, that we witness how isolation and despair can feed on one another, creating a downward spiral. In this chapter, we'll delve into how unacknowledged pain grows, the impact of unexpressed sorrow, and the importance of recognizing and addressing our struggles.

There is a powerful difference between experiencing pain and acknowledging it. Pain that is acknowledged, no matter how profound, begins the journey toward healing. When we name our pain, speak it, and allow ourselves to feel it fully, we take the first step toward release.

However, pain that is hidden or ignored only builds within us, like pressure in a closed container.

The pressure accumulates, intensifying with every unresolved disappointment, unspoken hurt, or unhealed trauma. Without an outlet, this contained pain can lead to feelings of despair, worthlessness, and sometimes even suicidal thoughts.

Many individuals who struggle with suicidal thoughts have found themselves unable to speak about the very things that weigh most heavily on their hearts. Perhaps they were told that sharing their feelings was a sign of weakness, or perhaps they feared judgment. In other cases, people feel a need to maintain an image of strength, hiding their pain even from those closest to them. But hiding these feelings does not make them disappear; rather, it amplifies their hold, feeding thoughts of loneliness and hopelessness.

Many people live have been lost as a result of unexpressed pain, I call them "the silent killers", I have over the years expressed to myself about my loses, as painful and as they were I had to vent at them, I use the Empty chair mostly with my clients to heal and recover. When disappointments, losses, and breakups are not processed or expressed, they become internalized. Each unacknowledged pain settles within, forming layer upon layer of unresolved sorrow. When this grief is not given voice, it often distorts an individual's sense of self-worth, feeding the inner critic that suggests they are not good enough, strong enough, or loved enough.

Over time, these internalized feelings can create a narrative of despair and self-doubt that is extremely difficult to escape.

For example, a person going through a painful breakup may feel lost, betrayed, or even worthless. Instead of expressing these emotions and seeking support, they may bottle it up, thinking it's something they should handle on their own. This isolation breeds a cycle of negative thoughts, leading them further into darkness. Without a release, pain festers and becomes toxic, corroding one's spirit. It convinces the individual that they are truly alone in their suffering, and that perhaps no one would understand, or worse, no one would care. This sense of isolation can feed into suicidal ideation, making it seem like the only option for relief.

If we are to break the cycle of unexpressed pain and the danger it poses, we must make room for connection and expression in our lives. Sharing our experiences and sorrows with others has a healing effect; it is in the sharing that we feel seen, understood, and, most importantly, not alone. Conversations with trusted friends, family, or mental health professionals provide a vital release. They can help reframe our perspectives, remind us of our worth, and show us that there is hope beyond our current pain.

Communities, too, play a critical role in this process. Encouraging open conversations about mental health, supporting each other, and being open to discussing life's struggles create spaces where individuals feel safe to express themselves.

We must cultivate environments where vulnerability is not stigmatized but celebrated as a sign of strength.

When we allow ourselves to truly acknowledge pain, we take a powerful step toward healing. It is in this acknowledgment that we break the silence, removing the hidden power pain has over us. Recognizing our suffering does not mean that it controls us; rather, it signals that we are ready to face it, accept it, and ultimately release it. By doing so, we reclaim our lives from the grip of despair and take back the narrative of our own existence.

Each day that we choose to express our pain and to lean on others for support is a day we build resilience against despair. Facing pain is a courageous act, one that reminds us of our inherent strength and our capacity to overcome even the darkest moments. In learning to share our burdens, we find that we are not alone; others have walked similar paths, felt similar sorrows, and together, we create a network of understanding and support.

22.
FROM SUFFERING TO STRENGTH

'I have learned things in pain that I could never have learned in joy.'
Wayne Muller

Some of life's most remarkable transformations emerge from the depths of suffering. When faced with intense hardship, certain individuals find a way not only to endure but to channel their pain into powerful sources of motivation, inspiration, and strength. This chapter shares stories of individuals who have navigated profound suffering and emerged stronger, illuminating the potential within each of us to turn adversity into an engine for growth and resilience. Their journeys reveal that, while suffering is universal, the ways we respond to it can define our legacy and impact in the world.

Finding Strength Through Adversity

For many, suffering becomes the impetus for profound self-discovery and inner strength. Take, for example, the story of Amara, a woman who faced the tragic loss of a child. In the depths of her grief, she found herself drawn to helping other parents navigate similar experiences. Through her support group, Amara not only found a sense of healing for herself but also created a space of hope and community for others. What once seemed an insurmountable pain became her purpose, enabling her to bring comfort and guidance to countless people who were also suffering.

Amara's story exemplifies how tragedy, though devastating, can give rise to strength and compassion that radiates outward to others.

Turning Pain into a Cause

For some, suffering spurs a call to action, as they channel their pain into causes that drive change. James, for instance, struggled for years with addiction and homelessness before he found his path to recovery. Once free from the grips of addiction, James dedicated himself to helping others overcome similar battles. His experience fueled his desire to advocate for accessible mental health services and addiction recovery programs. By sharing his story openly, James inspired those around him and became a voice for change, helping to reduce the stigma around addiction. His suffering became a source of empathy, strength, and commitment to a cause that now transforms lives.

Redefining Identity Through Hardship

Hardship can force us to rethink and redefine our identities, often revealing qualities we may not have previously known we possessed. Sofia, a cancer survivor, is powerful example of someone who turned a life-altering illness into a source of inner strength. Facing her diagnosis was one of the most terrifying moments of her life, but through her journey, she uncovered a fierce resilience and appreciation for life. After her recovery, Sofia began sharing her story publicly, reminding others of the importance of living fully and embracing life's fragility. Her experiences reshaped her identity, transforming her from a patient into a warrior, advocate, and inspiration for others on similar journeys.

Sofia's story demonstrates that suffering, though painful, can redefine who we are, revealing strengths, values, and passions that might have remained hidden otherwise. This transformation allows individuals to approach life with renewed purpose, gratitude, and a sense of clarity about what matters most.

The Power of Sharing Stories

Sharing our stories of suffering is an act of courage, one that has the power to inspire and connect. When Dev, a war veteran, returned home, he struggled with the invisible wounds of trauma. At first, he remained silent, fearing that sharing his experiences would isolate him even further. But eventually, he opened up about his journey, finding that his vulnerability resonated with others who had also endured trauma. His story became a source of hope, encouraging fellow veterans to seek healing and connection.

In sharing his story, Dev transformed his suffering into a source of strength, helping others see that they were not alone in their struggles. By being vulnerable, he created a bridge of empathy and support, turning his pain into a catalyst for collective healing and resilience.

Stories like Dev's show us that sharing our experiences not only helps us heal but also inspires those around us, creating a ripple effect of support and courage.

Using Suffering as a Source of Empathy

Suffering often deepens our empathy, allowing us to connect with others in a more profound way. Lily, a woman who grew up in extreme poverty, understands the daily struggles and silent fears that many people face. Her childhood experiences instilled in her a deep compassion for others, driving her to create a non-profit that provides resources and opportunities for children in underserved communities. Through her work, Lily empowers young people to pursue their dreams, offering them the support she longed for as a child.

Lily's journey exemplifies how suffering can cultivate empathy that leads to meaningful action. Her hardships became the foundation for her purpose, reminding us that even the most painful experiences can give rise to understanding, kindness, and a desire to make a difference. This empathy, born of suffering, is a testament to the resilience of the human spirit and the power of compassion.

Transforming Pain into Art

Art has long been a means of transforming pain into something meaningful and beautiful. Elijah, a musician, found solace in song writing during a period of intense depression and isolation. Pouring his emotions into music allowed him to process his pain and express feelings he could not put into words.

His music, which resonates with others who have experienced similar struggles, became a form of healing for himself and a source of comfort for his audience.

Elijah's story is a reminder that creative expression can be a pathway to healing. By transforming suffering into art, he not only navigated his own journey but also inspired others to find hope in their struggles. Art allows us to take our pain and turn it into something that transcends us, offering beauty, catharsis, and connection to those who experience it.

Lessons in Resilience and Purpose

These stories reveal that suffering, while challenging, can be a powerful force for good, uncovering hidden strengths, deepening empathy, and inspiring meaningful change. Each person's journey is a reminder that hardship need not define us solely as victims but as individuals capable of transformation and strength. By embracing their suffering and allowing it to guide them toward purpose, these individuals serve as examples of resilience, demonstrating that adversity can lead to some of life's most profound growth.

Whether through service, advocacy, art, or empathy, each person's story shows that it is possible to transform suffering into strength. By reframing pain as a tool for self-discovery and a source of purpose, we begin to see that our most challenging experiences can be the steppingstones to a more resilient, compassionate, and impactful life.

Final Reflections on Suffering as Strength

In the end, the stories of those who have turned suffering into strength inspire us to face our own challenges with hope and courage. They remind us that no pain is wasted if we can use it to inspire, connect, and uplift others. Suffering, while difficult, can lead us to our true purpose, allowing us to turn our darkest moments into sources of light for ourselves and the world around us.

May these stories of transformation encourage us to see our own hardships as opportunities for growth. Just as these individuals turned their pain into purpose, we too can embrace the potential within our suffering to build lives of resilience, compassion, and meaning. Through this perspective, we find strength not in spite of our pain but because of it, knowing that every challenge we overcome adds to the depth, empathy, and strength that we bring into the world.

23.
THE JOURNEY BEYOND PAIN

'Pain is the teacher no one wants but everyone needs.'
Unknown

Pain is an inevitable part of life, but it is also a remarkable teacher. Each hardship we face has the potential to lead us toward growth, resilience, and a deeper understanding of ourselves. The journey through pain is seldom easy, yet it is on this path that we discover our true strength. As we reflect on the experiences that have challenged us, we begin to see them not as roadblocks but as steppingstones to becoming the people we are meant to be.

Pain is a powerful force, shaping our lives in ways we rarely anticipate. It humbles us, reveals our vulnerabilities, and challenges our deepest beliefs about who we are and what we are capable of enduring. But beyond pain lies a place of profound transformation—a journey that leads us to resilience, wisdom, and a deeper understanding of ourselves and the world.

As we walk this path, we learn that pain, though often isolating, is also a bridge to others. It connects us to the shared experience of being human, reminding us that suffering and growth are universal. The courage to face our pain—and to let it teach us—opens our hearts to empathy, allowing us to approach others with compassion and understanding.

In this way, pain becomes a catalyst for meaningful relationships and a reminder that we are never truly alone.

Through this journey, we discover that we have the power to redefine pain's role in our lives. No longer merely a source of suffering, pain becomes a guide, illuminating the path toward growth, purpose, and authenticity. It encourages us to shed what no longer serves us and to embrace the person we are becoming.

Each hardship we face, each lesson we learn, leads us further along the journey beyond pain. And while pain will continue to be a part of life, we can carry forward the resilience, strength, and wisdom it has given us. We emerge not just as survivors but as transformed individuals, shaped by our experiences and ready to live with greater depth, compassion, and purpose.

As you close this book, may you carry with you the understanding that your pain has purpose, and may your journey forward be guided by the strength and wisdom you have earned. Pain may mark our past, but it does not have to define our future. Beyond pain lies growth, and in that growth, we find the truest versions of ourselves.

As we reach the end of this journey, it is clear that pain, though often an unwelcome visitor, has immense potential to foster growth, insight, and resilience. Pain challenges us to see ourselves more honestly, to shed the illusions we may hold, and to uncover strength we never knew we had.

Through each experience, we learn that we are capable of far more than we imagined—that we can not only survive but thrive.

Growth through pain is not a straightforward path; it is layered, often messy, and requires patience. It asks us to sit with discomfort, to seek meaning in what may seem meaningless, and to find courage in vulnerability. But through this process, we develop a deeper compassion for ourselves and for others, recognizing that every struggle, every setback, is a steppingstone on the path to self-discovery and fulfillment.

For those reading these pages, let this be an invitation to view your own struggles not as obstacles but as gateways. Each painful experience holds within it the seeds of transformation, the chance to become more fully and authentically yourself. Rather than letting pain define you, let it refine you, knowing that every step you take is a step toward a stronger, wiser, and more compassionate version of yourself.

As you move forward, carry with you the knowledge that pain is not an end, but a beginning. Each hardship is a teacher, each struggle a lesson, and each step forward an act of courage. May you find strength in your journey, and may you embrace every challenge as a powerful steppingstone toward a life of resilience, purpose, and peace.

Embracing Pain as a Path to Growth

Our struggles push us to confront parts of ourselves that might otherwise remain hidden. Pain invites us to examine our values, our beliefs, and our priorities, helping us to understand what truly matters. It strips away pretence, revealing the resilience we didn't know we had and teaching us lessons that often prove invaluable in the long run. With each difficult experience, we gain new insights, finding clarity in confusion, strength in weakness, and hope in despair.

Growth through pain doesn't happen overnight. It is a gradual, sometimes turbulent process that requires patience, self-compassion, and a willingness to keep moving forward. But as we embrace each experience as a steppingstone rather than an obstacle, we realize that pain, though uncomfortable, is a powerful catalyst for transformation.

Pain as a Source of Compassion and Connection

Pain is a universal experience, binding us to others in ways that few things can. When we embrace our own struggles, we gain the empathy to understand the challenges of those around us. This compassion connects us more deeply to others, reminding us that we are never alone in our hardships. It is often through our own healing that we feel called to help others, creating a ripple effect of kindness and support that transcends our individual experiences.

By viewing pain as an opportunity to connect with others, we shift from isolation to understanding. Our struggles, rather than setting us apart, become bridges that allow us to offer comfort and encouragement. In this way, our pain not only strengthens us but also enriches the lives of those we touch.

Transforming Struggles into Steppingstones

As we look back on the challenges we have overcome, we can begin to reframe our struggles as vital parts of our journey. Each setback, loss, or disappointment has brought us a step closer to who we are today. By viewing our pain as a steppingstone, we take ownership of our journey, recognizing that even the most painful moments have played a role in shaping us.

Seeing struggles as opportunities for growth empowers us to approach future challenges with resilience and confidence. It reminds us that no experience, no matter how difficult, is without value. Each challenge we face builds our inner strength, sharpens our purpose, and enhances our understanding of what it means to live fully.

Moving Forward with Purpose and Hope

As we conclude this journey of reflection, may we carry forward the lessons that pain has taught us. Let us approach each new challenge with a spirit of courage and an open heart, knowing that every experience, however difficult, can lead to growth.

By viewing our struggles as steppingstones, we transform pain from a source of suffering into a path of purpose and resilience.

Growth through pain is not just about survival—it is about thriving, finding meaning, and creating a life that reflects our deepest values and strengths. With this perspective, we find ourselves not defined by our hardships but empowered by them, stepping forward with hope, purpose, and the wisdom gained along the way.

May your journey beyond pain be one of transformation, strength, and fulfillment. And may you always remember that each step forward, however small, is a testament to the incredible resilience that resides within you.

24.
RAISING CHAMPIONS
(My life's commitment)

My thrust and drive in life is I strongly believe is, to raise life's champions in business, in entrepreneurs, in leadership, communities, and many areas of life's spheres. By raising champions through this book and many workshops and speaking platforms through the book, Taught and Schooled by Pain, shifts the focus, toward a vision of growth that encompasses not only individual resilience but also the nurturing of future generations to face life's challenges with courage and character. This involves exploring themes of how adversity shapes champions—not only in skill or strength but in heart, mindset, and values.

The world over in any given community, or area of skill in life, has proved that true champions—those who exhibit resilience, strength, and empathy—are often shaped not by moments of triumph alone but by the challenges and pain they've faced along the way. Pain acts as a crucible, forging character traits that cannot be developed through ease or comfort. In the context of pain, champions are defined by how they respond to adversity, transforming their suffering into wisdom and strength that extend beyond personal gain, often inspiring those around them.

When we being to look at pain as a crucial teacher for championship status requirement we will begin to enjoy and understand the peace that comes along with it.

Pain has an unparalleled capacity to teach lessons that shape a person's character deeply and enduringly. When faced with obstacles, setbacks, or personal loss, champions learn qualities like perseverance, humility, and emotional intelligence. They come to understand that greatness is not simply about external success but about the inner fortitude to continue in the face of hardship.

Through pain, champions also gain a sense of self-awareness and purpose. Adversity strips away illusions and superficial desires, leaving space to discover one's core values and strengths. This clarity enables them to set meaningful goals, focusing on what truly matters in their lives and pursuits.

Another key outcome of enduring pain is the development of empathy. Champions who have experienced hardship often have a heightened sensitivity to the struggles of others. This empathy fosters a connection with others and makes champions more effective leaders, teammates, and mentors. They become advocates for resilience, not just in themselves but in those they inspire, showing others that their struggles, too, can be a path to growth.

All champions in life are beacons of resilience, guiding lights for those who follow. They embody courage, selflessness, and an unwavering commitment to uplift others. Nelson Mandela showed us the power of forgiveness and the strength to endure in the face of immense adversity.

Mahatma Gandhi demonstrated the impact of peaceful resistance, leading a movement for justice through nonviolence. Mother Teresa taught the world compassion, dedicating her life to the care of the poor and marginalized. Florence Nightingale revolutionized healthcare with her devotion to those in need, transforming standards of care in the process.

Alongside these luminaries, there are many others who inspire us to push beyond our limits and embrace challenges. Martin Luther King Jr. championed civil rights with an unyielding commitment to equality, inspiring generations to stand up for justice. Helen Keller, despite her blindness and deafness, showed that the human spirit can overcome extraordinary obstacles, while Rosa Parks, with a single courageous act, helped ignite a movement for civil rights. Malala Yousafzai, even at a young age, risked her life to advocate for girls' education, reminding us that every voice matters. These and countless other champions demonstrate that resilience, love, and an unwavering faith in humanity can change the world. Their lives remind us that each of us has the power to be a beacon of hope and inspiration for others. In overcoming pain, champions also become beacons of resilience. Their stories of persistence in the face of adversity serve as powerful sources of motivation for others. When champions share their journeys, they reveal that pain is not something to be avoided at all costs but rather something to be acknowledged and used as a tool for personal and communal growth.

Champions are Purpose Drive because of Pain

Pain often becomes the driving force that propels champions toward their purpose. It reorients them toward goals and ambitions that align with their values. By enduring and growing through pain, they connect deeply with what they are meant to achieve, pursuing it with a sense of purpose that others can feel and draw strength from.

In Understanding Champions in the Context of Pain, we see that pain, rather than diminishing potential, actually lays the groundwork for greatness. It teaches life's most crucial lessons, building not only champions of strength but champions of the heart and mind. Through pain, these individuals emerge with resilience, humility, and purpose, embodying the truth that while pain may be inevitable, it also holds the power to cultivate champions who inspire change and hope in others.

Champions are often celebrated for their accomplishments and achievements, but seldom do we acknowledge the deeper, often painful, experiences that molded them. Pain becomes a mentor, teaching lessons that no traditional education can impart. Through challenges, setbacks, and personal struggles, champions cultivate qualities like perseverance, empathy, and mental fortitude—attributes that set them apart and empower them to make a meaningful impact on the world around them.

For those raising or mentoring young people, embracing the concept of 'taught and schooled by pain' means understanding how to foster resilience, adaptability, and compassion within them. Rather than shielding children or mentees from every hardship, this approach involves guiding them in facing and learning from difficulties. By doing so, they develop a foundation of strength that will serve them in all areas of life.

Empowering future generations to face life's inevitable challenges with resilience and grace is one of the most impactful gifts we can give. While we may wish to shield them from pain, it is through navigating hardship that young people build inner strength, empathy, and a sense of purpose. Empowering Future Generations in the context of pain involves guiding them to understand, embrace, and grow through the difficulties they encounter, fostering a mindset that turns obstacles into opportunities.

My experiences and many other's experiences in life has cultivated resilience in our lives and keeps inspiring many others to be resilient. Resilience—the ability to recover and adapt after setbacks—is not something that can be taught theoretically; it must be experienced.

By allowing young people to face and work through their struggles, they gain practical tools for managing life's challenges.

Rather than insulating them from all adversity, we can support them by helping them see setbacks as learning experiences and equipping them with the emotional and mental resources to persevere.

Through this process, they come to understand that failure and discomfort are temporary, while resilience is a lasting strength. This shift in perspective can help them approach future hardships with greater confidence and self-belief.

Pain is a powerful teacher of compassion—not only for oneself but for others. Empowering young people includes helping them develop self-compassion so they don't internalize hardship as a reflection of personal inadequacy. When young people learn to treat themselves kindly amid struggles, they are better equipped to handle failure and to see themselves as valuable regardless of the circumstances.

Additionally, experiencing and overcoming pain often increases empathy. Those who have been through hardship tend to be more understanding of others' suffering. This empathy enriches relationships and fosters a spirit of connectedness, which can be invaluable in personal and professional spheres.

Life's purposes are shaped and fostered through adversity. Pain and challenges can often act as catalysts for self-discovery, revealing what truly matters to us. Encouraging young people to reflect on their struggles allows them to identify their values and motivations, helping them move toward a sense of purpose.

Through adversity, you and me can come to understand who we are and what we want to contribute to the world.

With guidance, pain can clarify our paths, aligning our goals with a deeper sense of meaning.

Though adversity, while often very   painful, difficult to endure and unwelcome, has the potential to reveal profound insights and shape a powerful sense of purpose. Many people find their deepest motivations and aspirations forged in times of hardship, where life's challenges push them to re-evaluate their values and clarify what truly matters. Fostering Purpose Through Adversity explores how struggles, setbacks, and pain can lead individuals to discover meaningful directions for their lives.

Life's greatest purposes are often shaped and strengthened through adversity. Those who have faced profound challenges have found within themselves a deeper resolve, using their struggles to create meaningful change and leave a lasting impact on society. These individuals exemplify how hardship can foster strength, vision, and a commitment to a purpose far greater than themselves.

Nelson Mandela is a powerful example of this truth. After 27 years of imprisonment for his fight against apartheid, Mandela emerged with a spirit of forgiveness and unity that helped lead South Africa into a new era of democracy and racial reconciliation.

His legacy demonstrates that enduring hardship with grace can cultivate resilience and a lifelong commitment to justice.

Similarly, Malala Yousafzai faced life-threatening adversity at just 15, surviving an attack by extremists who opposed her advocacy for girls' education.

Instead of succumbing to fear, Malala emerged as a symbol of resilience, winning the Nobel Peace Prize and continuing to champion education worldwide. Her story reflects how the fight for justice is often born from personal trials.

Oprah Winfrey also exemplifies purpose shaped by adversity. Growing up in poverty and facing numerous challenges, she overcame abuse and hardship to become one of the most influential media figures in the world. Her story reveals that adversity, when met with determination, can foster empathy and a commitment to uplift others.

J.K. Rowling's journey to success was marked by poverty, rejection, and the pressures of single motherhood. Her perseverance in completing and publishing Harry Potter became a testament to the idea that great accomplishments often stem from enduring and pushing through life's most challenging periods.

Maya Angelou, the celebrated poet and activist, used her early experiences of hardship, discrimination, and abuse to inform her powerful writings.

Her works, filled with insight, resilience, and courage, continue to inspire generations. Angelou's life teaches us that personal pain can be transformed into wisdom that benefits others.

Even historical figures like Abraham Lincoln, who faced repeated failures, poverty, and deep personal losses, emerged as one of America's greatest leaders.

His resilience through adversity allowed him to guide the country through one of its darkest times, leaving an enduring legacy of unity and strength.

These individuals remind us that adversity, while painful, has the power to shape life's purpose in profound ways. When faced with hardship, those who choose resilience, compassion, and action can leave an impact on society that transcends their own struggles. They inspire us to see challenges not as obstacles but as powerful forces that can mould us into agents of change, capable of leaving the world better than we found it.

In times of struggle, we are often compelled to look inward, questioning who we are, what we stand for, and what we want out of life. This process of introspection helps us break down superficial goals and redefine our priorities. Adversity forces us to consider what is essential, often stripping away distractions and pushing us toward a more authentic version of ourselves.

By encouraging self-reflection, adversity becomes a catalyst for self-discovery.

As we confront and process difficult experiences, we gain insights into our strengths, limitations, and values. This clarity can help us identify a purpose aligned with who we truly are, rather than who we thought we should be.

Adversity, while often unwelcome, can serve as a powerful impetus for self-discovery, revealing parts of ourselves that might otherwise remain dormant.

When life is comfortable and predictable, we rarely have reason to question our motivations, values, or identity. But in times of struggle, adversity challenges us to reflect deeply, pushing us to uncover strengths, vulnerabilities, and passions we may not have known existed. In this sense, adversity can be a catalyst for discovering who we truly are and what matters most to us.

Pain teaches us to break the comfort zone and breaking it is embracing our success stories beyond our painful life`s experiences. Living life in the comfort zone is the quiet death of dreams, the place where potential fades, and where ambitions gradually lose their spark. The comfort zone offers a sense of security and familiarity, yet it quietly restrains growth and prevents the unfolding of our true capabilities. By choosing comfort over challenge, we often exchange daring for complacency, and as a result, our aspirations begin to wither.

In the comfort zone, dreams are suffocated, as it is here that we settle for 'good enough' instead of striving for greatness.

Skills that could be sharpened and expanded remain idle, and the potential that could be realized is left untouched.

When we allow ourselves to settle into comfort, we risk allowing our passions to become distant memories, trading future possibilities for present ease.

True growth lies in stepping beyond what is comfortable. It's in the willingness to face uncertainty, to take risks, and to challenge ourselves that we unlock our potential.

Embracing discomfort as a catalyst for development transforms not only our skills but also our outlook on life. Only by moving beyond the comfort zone do we allow ourselves to explore the full scope of what we're capable of achieving, creating a future that is driven by purpose, resilience, and courage. Adversity forces us out of our comfort zones, creating an environment where self-exploration becomes inevitable. When life feels secure, we often stick to what we know, following routines that don't require much introspection. However, adversity disrupts this, often shattering the illusion of control and compelling us to confront new realities. Through these challenges, we are pushed to question and redefine our assumptions about ourselves and the world around us. This upheaval often leads to profound insights about our values and priorities, helping us peel away superficial layers and get to the core of our identity.

One of the most transformative aspects of adversity is the way it reveals our inner strengths. Often, we are unaware of our resilience until we are required to tap into it.

Through hardship, we discover qualities like perseverance, patience, and courage, all of which might have remained hidden if not for the adversity we faced. As we navigate challenges, we learn to appreciate these qualities within ourselves, fostering a sense of self-worth and confidence that transcends the hardships.

The strengths revealed in times of struggle also change how we perceive future challenges.

By recognizing our capacity to overcome adversity, we develop a resilient mindset that empowers us to face new difficulties with less fear and more trust in our ability to endure.

Adversity often brings heightened self-awareness. Pain, loss, and failure create moments where we're forced to pause, reflect, and re-evaluate our lives. In these moments, we may ask questions like, 'Who am I without this role or achievement?' or 'What do I truly want out of life?' Such self-inquiry is rarely comfortable, but it allows us to see ourselves more honestly. This process of self-awareness helps us identify our values, beliefs, and goals with clarity, enabling us to align our lives more closely with what truly matters to us.

Many people find their sense of purpose during times of adversity. As hardship prompts us to look inward, we often come to understand what brings us fulfillment and what values we hold most dear.

This clarity can inspire us to pursue paths that reflect our newfound understanding, whether by changing careers, deepening relationships, or engaging in meaningful community work. When we recognize that our struggles have meaning, they become sources of motivation rather than obstacles, guiding us toward a life aligned with our deeper purpose.

Adversity not only reveals things about ourselves but also fosters empathy and connection with others. Through personal struggles, we gain insight into the pain of others, deepening our compassion and understanding. This empathy can strengthen our relationships, enabling us to connect more meaningfully with those around us. In this way, self-discovery through adversity becomes a shared journey, where our own pain fosters a sense of connection and community that enhances our personal growth.

As we navigate adversity, we often find ourselves shedding layers of inauthenticity. The pressures to conform or seek approval may diminish in the face of hardship, freeing us to embrace our true selves. Adversity clarifies what we stand for and what no longer serves us, allowing us to live with greater authenticity and integrity. By becoming more comfortable with vulnerability, we begin to accept our flaws, celebrate our strengths, and embrace who we are without apology.

Ultimately, adversity serves as a foundation for ongoing self-discovery and growth.

The lessons learned from hardship do not disappear when challenges fade; they become part of who we are. Every experience of pain and resilience adds layers to our identity, equipping us with insights and skills that prepare us for the future.

In Adversity as a Catalyst for Self-Discovery, we learn that while hardship may feel isolated, it also provides unique opportunities to explore our innermost selves. Through adversity, we uncover strengths, values, and passions that define us, helping us navigate life with a deeper understanding and acceptance of who we are. This self-discovery transforms adversity from a burden into a gift, teaching us that even in our darkest moments, we are capable of profound growth and self-realization.

Transforming Pain into a Driving Force

Pain, when processed constructively, can be a powerful source of motivation.

Many individuals who have faced loss, trauma, or setbacks channel their experiences into endeavors' that prevent others from enduring similar struggles. This desire to make a difference often defines purpose, as individuals use their pain to fuel their passions and create positive change.

For example, people who have faced illness may advocate for medical research; those who have experienced loss may work to support grieving individuals.

In these ways, pain is transformed into purpose, turning personal adversity into a drive that benefits not only oneself but also the broader community.

Finding Meaning in Service to Others

One of the most powerful aspects of purpose is its potential to extend beyond the individual. Many who have endured hardship find purpose in serving others, using their experiences to uplift and support those on similar paths. This outward focus helps reframe personal struggles as sources of connection and empathy, turning pain into a bridge rather than a barrier.

By helping others, we gain a sense of fulfillment that often feels deeper than accomplishments achieved solely for ourselves. Service enables us to see the value in our struggles as we realize that our experiences can bring comfort, strength, and encouragement to others.

Purpose derived from adversity often leaves a lasting legacy—a story of resilience, courage, and growth that inspires future generations. When individuals find purpose in their pain, they become role models for how to transform life's hardships into sources of strength.

Their stories demonstrate that while adversity may change us, it does not have to break us; instead, it can shape us into more purposeful and impactful individuals.

Building a Growth Mindset

Empowering future generations involves instilling a growth mindset—the belief that abilities and intelligence can be developed through dedication and effort. When young people view pain as an opportunity to grow, rather than a dead end, they learn to approach challenges with curiosity and resilience. Encouraging them to ask questions like, 'What can I learn from this?' and 'How can this make me stronger?' allows them to see pain not as a failure but as part of their ongoing development.

Being Role Models of Strength and Vulnerability

As mentors, parents, teachers, and caregivers, our role is not to remove pain from their path but to model strength and vulnerability. By showing how we confront and learn from our own struggles, we provide a blueprint for handling life's challenges.

When young people see those adults, too, face hardship and emerge stronger, they gain confidence that they, too, can rise from pain.

Creating a Supportive Environment

Empowering future generations also means building a supportive environment where they feel safe to express their struggles. This environment allows them to be vulnerable, ask for help, and feel understood. With the foundation of a compassionate support system, they are more likely to embrace pain as part of their journey rather than something to be avoided or hidden.

In Empowering Future Generations, we can guide young people to see pain not as a punishment or flaw but as a powerful, transformative force. This empowerment teaches them to build strength from within, face challenges with resilience, and ultimately to emerge as compassionate, self-aware individuals who are prepared not only to overcome their own challenges but to make a positive impact on the world around them.

Pain as the Path to Purpose

The journey of becoming a champion—whether in personal growth, leadership, or skill—is often forged in times of trial. Pain can reveal a person's purpose by stripping away superficial goals and focusing the mind on what truly matters. This path encourages individuals to transcend their circumstances, find clarity amid adversity, and connect deeply with their own values and strengths.

In the narrative of Raising Champions: Taught and Schooled by Pain, you are encouraged to view the hardships

they encounter, and those faced by the young people they mentor, as steppingstones toward greatness. This perspective teaches that while pain is inevitable, the choice to learn and grow from it is what ultimately defines a champion.

The book serves as both a guide and an inspiration for individuals and caregivers alike, underscoring the transformative power of pain in shaping resilient, compassionate, and purpose-driven champions.

The pain of my mother's death was overwhelming, a loss that shook me deeply. Losing my brothers in the years that followed compounded that grief, each loss tearing a piece of my heart. Then came the breaking of my relationship with Jordan's mother, a painful separation that felt like being cut by a blunt knife—slow and jagged. Though we weren't married, the ending of that relationship felt like a profound loss, stirring emotions I had not anticipated and amplifying the weight of past sorrows. Each of these moments, marked by deep and lingering pain, seemed like insurmountable obstacles at the time.

But these painful chapters became the soil in which my determination was planted. In the darkness of each loss, I found a growing resolve to achieve, to succeed, and, most importantly, to discover a purpose that felt meaningful.

Life's most challenging experiences have a way of distilling our focus, stripping away the trivial, and revealing what truly matters. As I navigated the waves of grief and disappointment,

I realized that purpose is often tucked away within life's most difficult trials, waiting to be discovered and nurtured.

Through these hardships, I found that pain can be a powerful motivator, urging us to rise, to build, and to shape lives that honor the resilience we develop along the way. I became relentless in the pursuit of my goals, driven by the belief that within every setback lies the seed of a comeback. Life's difficulties did not diminish me; instead, they stirred a fire within to find meaning in the struggle, to make my life a testament to resilience, and to use my experiences as fuel for growth and purpose.

Pain, though often feared and resisted, has a remarkable ability to reveal purpose. It strips away the superficial, confronts us with our vulnerabilities, and compels us to seek deeper meaning.

When we process and channel pain constructively, it becomes a powerful source of motivation, shaping a life aligned with our values and aspirations. Pain as the Fuel for Purpose explores how hardship, rather than an obstacle, can propel us toward fulfilling our true potential and living with intentionality.

In this journey of life, I discovered that greatness often emerges from the deepest wounds, and that fulfillment is found not in avoiding pain but in allowing it to sharpen our focus and shape our resolve. Pain has a way of becoming purpose, and it is through embracing life's most difficult experiences that we unlock the strength to pursue our dreams with tenacity and clarity.

Transforming Pain into Motivation

When pain disrupts our lives, it challenges us to look for meaning beyond the suffering. This search often fuels a drive

to improve our circumstances, pushing us to pursue goals and ambitions that feel purposeful.

Pain, when understood and integrated, can create a sense of urgency, reminding us of life's impermanence and inspiring us to focus on what genuinely matters. This motivation doesn't diminish as time passes; instead, it becomes a constant source of energy that propels us forward, allowing us to transcend the limitations imposed by hardship.

Pain has a unique ability to clarify our values and priorities. During periods of adversity, we are often forced to reassess what is essential and meaningful in our lives.

This process of introspection can illuminate our values, shaping a vision of purpose grounded in authenticity. By confronting and understanding our pain, we gain clarity about who we are and what we stand for, helping us align our lives with our deepest convictions.

This clarity transforms our struggles into a compass, guiding us toward pursuits and relationships that reflect our true selves. Instead of avoiding pain, we learn to listen to it, using it as a tool to recalibrate our goals and make choices that honor our values.

One way or the other we all experience pain, loss, grief and life's turbulences. Many individuals who experience deep pain feel compelled to turn their suffering into service.

Pain fosters empathy and compassion, connecting us to the struggles of others. This sense of connection often fuels a desire to make a positive impact, to prevent others from enduring similar hardships, or to support those who are suffering. When we channel our pain into helping others, we give it a purpose beyond ourselves, transforming it from a burden into a means of making a difference.

After the painful breakup with my ex, I found myself struggling to cope with life. I had loved her deeply, and her absence left a significant void. In search of purpose and solace, I turned my attention to working with children, teaching and coaching them in various sporting activities.

This endeavor became a form of service that not only allowed me to give back but also helped me redefine my own sense of worth. I have always loved children, and immersing myself in their lives became a pivotal experience for me.

During this time, I also faced the heartache of being separated from my children, which meant I couldn't see them for long stretches. This separation intensified my feelings of loss and longing, making my journey even more challenging. However, I found healing by channeling my pain into a commitment to help less privileged children. In those children, I saw reflections of my love for Jordan. Each interaction became a way for me to connect with my emotions, to honor what I had lost by being there for others in need.

I often volunteered at an orphanage, where I poured my heart into the lives of the children.

There were times when I would return to my room and cry uncontrollably, the weight of my sorrow overwhelming me. Yet, deep down, I understood that this emotional release was a part of my healing process. Working with those children served as a form of surgical healing, allowing me to confront my pain while transforming it into something

meaningful. Through my service, I discovered not only a way to cope but also a renewed sense of purpose—one that connected my past experiences with a brighter, more hopeful future.

This outward focus enables us to find purpose through service, creating meaning in our lives and making our own pain feel purposeful. Whether it's through advocacy, mentorship, or charity, serving others becomes a way to honor our experiences and use them to create positive change.

Your Strength is in being Vulnerable

The journey of purpose is not about masking pain but embracing it as part of who we are. Vulnerability, often perceived as weakness, becomes a strength when we allow it to fuel our purpose. By sharing our experiences openly, we create spaces where others feel seen and understood, fostering genuine connections that are grounded in empathy. This authenticity inspires us to pursue paths that resonate deeply with our true selves, reinforcing our purpose and strengthening our resolve.

When we embrace our pain rather than hide it, we find that vulnerability enhances our purpose.

It empowers us to show up fully, drawing strength from the parts of ourselves that once seemed fragile.

Nurture Resilience and Grit in your Painful Moments

Tell me about it yes, "Pain builds resilience and grit—qualities essential for a purpose-driven life." When we navigate pain and emerge on the other side, we develop an inner fortitude that fuels us through challenges.

This resilience makes us less likely to be deterred by setbacks, enabling us to approach our goals with courage and determination. By learning to persevere through hardship, we build the mental and emotional endurance needed to pursue our purpose, regardless of the obstacles we encounter.

Resilience teaches us that pain is not the end but rather part of the journey, a reminder that even in our lowest moments, we have the strength to continue moving forward.

Through pain, we often redefine our concept of success. The experiences that test us reveal that success is not solely about external accomplishments but also about the impact we have on others and the sense of fulfillment we derive from our choices. Pain teaches us to value meaningful experiences, lasting connections, and contributions that align with our purpose, encouraging us to build a legacy that reflects our journey.

In redefining success, we shift our focus from fleeting achievements to a purpose that endures, one rooted in the wisdom and strength we've gained from our struggles.

Pain, when used as fuel for purpose, becomes a source of growth rather than defeat. It pushes us to evolve, inspiring us to seek opportunities for self-improvement, healing, and transformation. As we grow, our sense of purpose deepens, becoming intertwined with our identity and shaping how we engage with the world. This growth-oriented approach to pain allows us to view life's difficulties not as setbacks but as steppingstones toward a purposeful existence.

In Pain is the most powerful fuel to achieving purpose in life, we learn that adversity, while challenging, offers

profound opportunities to connect with our true calling. Through the lessons of hardship, we gain clarity, empathy, resilience, and a sense of mission that enriches our lives and the lives of those we touch. Pain, rather than something to be avoided, becomes a powerful catalyst for discovering, defining, and pursuing our purpose, transforming our struggles into a source of strength, meaning, and legacy.

Unacknowledged pain can be a dangerous and silent force, feeding into despair and even leading to suicide if left unaddressed. By recognizing and expressing our struggles, we interrupt this cycle, allowing ourselves to experience life's full range of emotions without shame or fear.

Through honest conversation, connection, and support, we gain the tools to not only survive but thrive, transforming pain into strength and resilience.

In the end, it is the shared stories, the open conversations, and the willingness to confront our sorrows that allow us.

25.
TAUGHT AND SCHOOLED BY PAIN
(While Waiting for The Promise)

Abraham's life illustrates the journey of faith and the complexities of waiting on God. While he was promised a son through whom he would become the father of many nations, the prolonged delay led to moments of doubt and detours. One such moment was the birth of Ishmael—a decision that brought its own challenges and lessons.

The Pain of Delay and the Struggle to Trust

When God initially promised Abraham that he would be the father of a great nation, Abraham was already advanced in years, and his wife Sarah was barren. As years passed with no child, both Abraham and Sarah wrestled with their hopes and doubts. Waiting in faith was painful; every passing year seemed to test the limits of their patience and trust. Overwhelmed by the silence and the impossibility of the situation, they wondered if perhaps God's promise required their intervention.

Ishmael: A Painful Detour

In a moment of doubt, Sarah proposed that Abraham take Hagar, her Egyptian servant, to conceive a child. Following Sarah's suggestion, Abraham's fathered a son, Ishmael, through Hagar. But this decision led to complex and painful consequences. Tension arose between Sarah and Hagar, leading to bitterness, jealousy, and strife in Abraham's household.

While Ishmael was a blessing in his own right, this choice was not God's intended path for fulfilling His covenant with Abraham.

This painful detour taught Abraham that attempting to fulfill God's promises through human means can lead to unintended heartache and challenges. Ishmael's birth became a reminder of the consequences of stepping out of alignment with God's plan, especially when the way forward seems uncertain.

God's Faithfulness Despite the Detour

Despite this setback, God reaffirmed His promise to Abraham. He clarified that Sarah would indeed bear a son, Isaac, through whom His covenant would be established. Though Ishmael would be blessed and become the father of a great nation, God's covenantal promise remained tied to Isaac, the son of faith rather than human intervention.
Through this process, Abraham learned the depth of God's grace and patience. Even when human actions complicate the journey, God's faithfulness endures. Abraham's waiting became a schooling in faith and surrender, a lesson that the fulfillment of divine promises lies in God's timing and power, not human planning.

Lessons from Abraham's Waiting

Abraham's experience reveals the value of trusting God fully, especially when facing delays and uncertainty. Though his journey involved missteps, it ultimately reinforced his dependence on God's faithfulness.

Waiting on God requires patience, humility, and surrender—qualities Abraham was shaped by, even through his mistakes.

This chapter of Abraham's life teaches us that even when we falter, God can redeem our choices and bring forth His promises. Abraham's story is a reminder that true fulfillment comes from aligning with God's purpose and timing, trusting that He is faithful to bring His promises to fruition, even after seasons of pain and waiting.

26.
THE PAIN OF DELAY

When Waiting Gives Birth to Lifelong Challenges

In life, the pain of delay can be one of the most agonizing experiences. When hopes seem deferred and promises remain unfulfilled, frustration and impatience often rise. We may feel tempted to take matters into our own hands, seeking shortcuts or solutions that may offer temporary relief but lead to lasting complications. Taught and schooled by pain, this chapter examines how impatience can birth challenges that linger for a lifetime.

Impatience and Its Lifelong Consequences

The story of Abraham is a powerful example of how acting from a place of impatience can lead to unintended and far-reaching consequences. When God promised Abraham he would father a nation, years passed without a child. In his and Sarah's discouragement, they turned to a solution of their own making, which led to the birth of Ishmael. While Ishmael himself was a blessing, the situation brought strife and division within Abraham's family, resulting in a lifetime of challenges and fractured relationships.

This experience shows that when we try to rush processes meant to unfold in their own time, we can inadvertently create situations that are difficult to undo, carrying consequences we may not have foreseen.

How Delays Shape Character

The pain of waiting, while challenging, is often intended to shape our character, fostering patience, humility, and resilience. But if we sidestep these lessons in favor of a quicker outcome, we may miss the deeper transformation that waiting produces. The struggles of delayed gratification teach us the importance of trust, especially when circumstances seem discouraging.

When we learn to wait, we become stronger, more resilient, and better prepared for what lies ahead. In contrast, when we take shortcuts out of impatience or desperation, we often bring about results that bring long-term complications, undermining the very fulfillment we sought.

Lessons in Surrender and Trust

Waiting periods call us to surrender, to place our desires and dreams fully in God's hands and trust His timing. While delays can feel painful and isolated, they also offer opportunities for reflection, growth, and realignment. In waiting, we deepen our relationship with God, finding strength in His promises and guidance instead of our own plans. Learning to embrace the waiting allows us to avoid the costly mistakes that may arise from impatience.

Moving Forward with Wisdom

The pain of delay is never easy, but it is often a refining fire, intended to produce wisdom, maturity, and faith. Embracing the waiting process can open us to greater clarity and peace, helping us avoid choices that may yield unintended, lifelong challenges. This chapter of being taught and schooled by pain reminds us that while delay may be painful, it is also purposeful. With patience and trust, we can emerge stronger, more resilient, and ready for the fulfillment that awaits us—without the unnecessary baggage of avoidable hardships.

The Purposefulness of Painful Delay

Painful delays often come as unwelcome interruptions in our lives. They test our patience, shake our resolve, and challenge our understanding. Yet even the most agonizing delays are purposeful, carrying within them hidden blessings and opportunities for profound growth. When we endure seasons of waiting, we are given a unique chance to cultivate patience, deepen our resilience, and refine our focus on what truly matters.

The Refining Power of Waiting

Delays invite us to step back, assess our intentions, and build the character needed for what lies ahead. They shape us in ways that only time and patience can, fostering humility, gratitude, and the quiet strength to persevere.

In waiting, we learn the power of trust, of surrendering control to a greater plan that often exceeds our immediate understanding. This refining process is what prepares us for the depth and responsibility of future blessings.

Aligning with a Greater Plan

When we experience painful delays, it is an opportunity to realign our goals with a purpose that may be greater than our own. Delays encourage us to look beyond ourselves, to find meaning in service, and to appreciate the journey rather than rush to the destination. The waiting period draws us closer to a place of clarity and wisdom, showing us what we may have missed in a rush.

A Promise in the Delay

Every delay holds a promise—it is a reminder that what is worth having is worth waiting for. Through the struggles and setbacks, we become prepared for the responsibility and joy that awaits. The delay becomes not a denial, but a detour meant to bring us closer to our purpose.

In the end, painful delays remind us that timing is as important as the blessing itself. By embracing the waiting, we learn that life's delays are not random but purposeful, leading us to an understanding of life, purpose, and grace that only the journey of waiting can provide.

27.
AGAINST HOPE, ABRAHAM BELIEVED IN HOPE

The story of Abraham is a profound testament to the power of hope and faith, particularly in the face of seemingly insurmountable obstacles. Against all odds, Abraham chose to believe in hope, even when circumstances offered him no tangible reason to do so. This remarkable choice serves as a powerful reminder of the strength of conviction and the unwavering belief in the promises of God.

When God made a covenant with Abraham, promising him descendants as numerous as the stars in the sky, the reality of Abraham's situation was starkly different. At an advanced age, with his wife Sarah equally barren and beyond childbearing years, there was little in their lives that suggested the fulfilment of such a promise. The weight of their circumstances could have easily led them to despair, yet Abraham's faith transcended the physical evidence around him. He chose to hope against hope.

This choice to believe in the ability of God to fulfil His promises highlight a crucial aspect of faith: it often requires us to look beyond our current realities. Abraham's faith was not rooted in what he could see or feel, but in the unwavering conviction that God is faithful and capable of bringing to fruition what He has declared.

This act of faith is a powerful lesson for us all, teaching us that hope is not merely a passive expectation but an active decision to trust in God's character and His word.

In moments of doubt and uncertainty, we can draw strength from Abraham's example. His life illustrates that hope is not contingent upon our circumstances but rather on the promises of God. When we face challenges that seem insurmountable, we are invited to embrace a similar faith—a faith that persists in believing, even when everything around us suggests otherwise.

Abraham's journey encourages us to cultivate hope, reminding us that, despite the odds, God remains faithful to His promises. Just as Abraham held onto hope, we too can choose to believe in the possibilities that lie ahead. This belief can ignite a profound transformation in our lives, empowering us to move forward with courage and determination. Against all hope, we can find hope—rooted in faith and anchored in the assurance that God is always at work, fulfilling His promises in our lives.

In the Turning Around – From Victim to Survivor: Taught and Schooled by Pain is a testament to the strength of the human spirit. Through pain, we can learn invaluable lessons that shape us into resilient, purpose-driven individuals. Each lesson serves as a stepping stone on the path to healing, empowering us to transform our lives and the lives of those around us. The journey is not easy, but it is one filled with growth, connection, and hope.to find hope again. Our pain becomes part of our journey, not as a source of despair, but as a testament to our capacity for growth, healing, and ultimately, joy.

28.
ACCOUNTABILITY

Accountability is the bridge between our actions and their consequences. In the journey through pain, taking responsibility for our choices becomes a critical step in personal growth and transformation. Pain has a unique way of teaching us to own our stories—not just the victories but also the failures, regrets, and shortcomings.

To be accountable is to confront the truth of our actions, no matter how uncomfortable, and to recognize how those actions have shaped our lives and impacted others. It is an invitation to step out of victimhood and into empowerment, understanding that while we may not control everything that happens to us, we can always control our responses.

In this final chapter, I write deep about the power of accountability as a transformative force. It explores how pain can teach us to reflect, adjust, and grow. Through real-life examples and practical guidance, readers are encouraged to take responsibility for their healing and to embrace the lessons pain has to offer.

The Role Accountability Plays in one's Healing

Life often presents us with challenges that shake us to our core—moments of pain, disappointment, and heartbreak that can leave us feeling powerless and adrift. These experiences, though painful, hold an inherent truth: while we cannot control what happens to us, we can control how we respond to it. A critical step in this journey is accountability—not to others alone but to ourselves. It is through this lens of self-accountability that healing begins, freedom takes root, and transformation becomes possible.

Understanding Accountability

Accountability is often misunderstood as something owed to others—our families, employers, or communities. While external accountability has its place, true accountability starts within. It is a commitment to ourselves to take responsibility for our actions, decisions, and the trajectory of our lives, even in the face of pain and adversity.

When we are accountable to ourselves, we acknowledge our role in our healing process. It is an act of empowerment. Pain may have knocked us down, but self-accountability is the decision to rise again. It is the refusal to remain a victim of circumstances and instead become an active participant in our recovery and growth.

Accountability and the Healing Journey

Healing is not a passive process. It demands deliberate effort, courage, and self-reflection. Accountability requires us to: You and me have got to get involved willingly and committedly.

Own our Choices

Painful experiences often lead us to make decisions fueled by anger, fear, or despair. Whether it's lashing out, withdrawing, or making unwise choices, these actions stem from our pain. Accountability challenges us to examine these responses, own them, and choose differently moving forward.

Let Go of the Blame Game

It is natural to seek someone or something to blame for our suffering. While assigning blame might offer temporary relief, it doesn't heal us. Accountability shifts the focus from what others did to us to what we can do for ourselves. It is the bridge from bitterness to liberation.

Set Clear Intentions

Accountability demands clarity about what we want for ourselves—peace, freedom, or fulfillment. It calls us to set intentions and take actions that align with these desires. Healing begins when we stop drifting and start navigating life with purpose.

Embrace Honest Reflections

Healing through accountability means we regularly pause to assess our progress, setbacks, and growth. Are we moving toward healing, or are we stuck in patterns that prolong our pain? This honesty with ourselves, though uncomfortable, is transformative.

The Power of Accountability Despite Pain

Accountability does not mean ignoring or suppressing the pain we've endured. Instead, it is about choosing to confront that pain with a sense of ownership. Here's why accountability is vital even when life has been unkind:

It Restores Control

When we take responsibility for our healing, we reclaim control over our lives. Pain no longer defines us; instead, we define how we rise from it.

It Builds Resilience

Accountability teaches us to endure and grow. Each step we take toward accountability strengthens our resolve and prepares us for future challenges.

It Fosters Self-Respect

When we honor our role in our healing, we build a deeper sense of self-respect. This respect is the foundation for healthier relationships and a more fulfilling life.

It Opens Doors to your Freedom

True freedom comes when we release the weight of blame, guilt, and shame. Accountability helps us shed these burdens and step into a life of peace and purpose.

PRACTICAL STEPS TO EMBRACE ACCOUNTABILITY

1. Acknowledge your Pain

Healing starts with honesty. Admit where you are hurting and how it has affected your decisions and actions.

2. Define your Goals

What does heal look like for you? Be specific. Whether it's regaining confidence, rebuilding trust, or finding joy, clarity will guide your journey.

3. Create an Action Plan

Break your goals into actionable steps. What can you do daily, weekly, or monthly to move toward healing?

4. Seek Support

While accountability starts within, it doesn't mean you must walk the journey alone. Trusted friends, mentors, or counsellors can provide encouragement and perspective.

5. Celebrate Progress

Healing is a process, not a destination. Acknowledge and celebrate each step forward, no matter how small.

A Cloosing Invitation

Pain can teach us, shape us, and propel us into a future we never imagined. But only if we take responsibility for our part in the journey. Accountability is not about perfection; it's about progress.

It's about owning our story—not just the pain but the healing, growth, and triumph that come after.

As you move forward, remember this truth: the path to healing and freedom begins with you. You are the author of your life. Take the pen, write a new chapter, and hold yourself accountable to live it well.

Accountability: Stand Up, Learn, and Move On

Life's trials often leave us battered, wounded, and struggling to find our footing. It is natural to feel overwhelmed, to want to retreat into the comfort of self-pity, and to dwell on the injustices of our circumstances. But here's the hard truth: staying in that place of licking your wounds, whining, and blaming others will not bring healing. It only traps you in a cycle of stagnation.

Healing begins when we choose to stand up, face the reality of our pain, and take accountability—not just for what has happened, but for our response to it. It is not about ignoring the wrongs done to us or pretending our pain doesn't matter. It's about recognizing our role in the story, learning the lessons, and taking the steps to move forward.

The Trap of Blame and Victimhood

Blame is an easy place to hide when life becomes difficult. It feels justified to point fingers at others—the people who hurt us, the circumstances that crushed us, or even fate itself. But blame has a dangerous side effect: it keeps us stuck.

When we focus solely on what others have done, we surrender our power. Blame turns our pain into a prison, locking us into the role of the victim. It may offer temporary solace, but it doesn't bring healing. In fact, it prolongs our suffering by keeping us fixated on the past instead of moving toward the future.

The Courage to be Accountable

Accountability is not about excusing the actions of those who wronged us. It's about taking ownership of what we can control—our choices, our mindset, and our healing journey. It requires courage to say, *'Yes, I've been hurt, but I also have a role to play in how I respond.'*
Being accountable means admitting the ways we may have contributed to our situation. Did we ignore warning signs? Did we make choices that led to unintended consequences? Did we react in ways that deepened our pain? Accountability forces us to confront these questions honestly—not to judge ourselves harshly, but to grow.

The Lessons in Pain

Every painful experience carries a lesson if we are willing to learn. Accountability helps us uncover these lessons. It shifts our perspective from asking, *'Why did this happen to me?'* to *'What can I learn from this?'*

Self-Awareness: Pain reveals our vulnerabilities, patterns, and triggers. Accountability allows us to examine these areas and make changes where needed.

Growth: The lessons of pain often push us to grow in ways we wouldn't have chosen voluntarily. Accountability transforms our struggles into opportunities for development.

Wisdom: When we learn from our experiences, we gain the wisdom to navigate future challenges with greater clarity and resilience.

Moving on: The Path to your Healing

Moving on doesn't mean forgetting what happened or pretending it didn't hurt. It means refusing to let the pain define us. It is about making the conscious decision to rise above, to reclaim our lives, and to walk into healing with purpose.

Take Responsibility

Accepting responsibility for our part in the situation doesn't diminish the wrongs of others. It simply acknowledges our power to influence our healing.

Release the Past

Accountability requires letting go of what we cannot change. Holding on to anger, regret, or resentment only weighs us down.

Focus on Action

Healing isn't just an emotional process—it's a practical one. What steps can you take today to move forward? Seek therapy, mend broken relationships, or start pursuing your goals again.

Be Honest with Yourself

Accountability means being real about where you are and

what you need. Denial will only delay the process. Embrace your truth, no matter how messy it feels.

Cultivate Gratitude

Even in pain, there are things to be thankful for. Gratitude shifts our focus from what we've lost to what we still have.

The Power of Moving Forward

Standing up and taking accountability doesn't mean the journey will be easy. There will be moments of doubt, fear, and even setbacks. But with every step forward, you reclaim your strength and your story.

By learning the lessons pain teaches, you not only heal yourself but also become a source of inspiration for others. Accountability transforms us from victims to victors, from wounded to wise. It is the foundation for a life that is not just survived but thrived.

A Final Word

Pain may have entered your life without your permission, but healing requires your participation. Stop licking your wounds. Stop whining, complaining, or blaming others for what has happened.

Stand up. Be Accountable. Learn the lessons. Move on.

This is not just about overcoming what hurt you—it's about discovering the strength, wisdom, and resilience that were within you all along. Your healing is your responsibility, and your freedom is within reach.

Take the first step today.

BIBLICAL LESSONS ON RESILIENCE

A Desire to Succeed and the Drive to Overcome Setbacks

In our journey of faith and personal growth, the Bible provides countless stories of individuals who faced overwhelming setbacks yet demonstrated an unwavering desire to succeed and fulfil their God-given purpose. The stories of Joseph, David, and the Apostle Paul remind us that success and resilience are inseparable; they require a heart that trusts God through every trial, and a mindset that sees challenges as steps toward victory.

Joseph: Rising Above Injustice

Joseph's story is a classic biblical example of resilience born out of a deep-seated desire to fulfil his purpose. Sold into slavery by his own brothers and later wrongfully imprisoned, Joseph could have surrendered to despair. Yet, he maintained his faith in God, trusting that his life had purpose beyond the setbacks he faced. Years later, Joseph's resilience led to his position as a leader in Egypt, where he not only found success but also saved many lives, including those of his own family (Genesis 37–50).

David: Defeating the Giants

David's journey—from shepherd boy to king—highlights the power of trusting God while facing enormous challenges. Before his rise to the throne, David encountered a giant, Goliath, an obstacle that should have stopped him. But his courage and reliance on God's strength allowed him to overcome the impossible. His life, marked by triumphs and failures, teaches us that resilience is often built on our commitment to keep moving forward, despite our setbacks and weaknesses (1 Samuel 17).

Paul: Persevering for a Greater Cause

The Apostle Paul endured imprisonment, beatings, and countless hardships for the sake of the Gospel. His resilience was fuelled by a mission far greater than himself—spreading the message of Christ. In his letters, Paul often encouraged others to persevere, writing, *'I can do all things through Christ who strengthens me'* (Philippians 4:13). Paul's life is a reminder that even in the face of adversity, our desire to succeed in our calling, combined with faith, can carry us through any hardship.

Moving Forward with Resilience

True success in overcoming setbacks comes from placing our trust in God, finding purpose in our trials, and allowing Him to refine us through them. Resilience means learning to see beyond the present pain, believing in a greater outcome that only God can fully envision. As we choose faith over fear and purpose over despair, we find ourselves stepping into the victorious life God has prepared for us. In this way, we are taught and schooled by pain, discovering that resilience is both a choice and a gift.

This chapter, inspired by these biblical examples, invites you to harness your own desire to succeed—one that is rooted in faith, and powered by an unyielding drive to overcome.

My Message to all Life's Champions & Champions in the Making!

The painful experiences, losses, heartbreaks, and moments of deep sorrow etched into my life's journey have been transformative, shaping me into the tenacious champion I am today. These challenges, indelibly marked in my memory, have taught me resilience, strength, and the will to press forward regardless of the obstacles.

Every setback and each hardship in my life has been a lesson, molding me into someone who refuses to be denied the accomplishment of my goals. This book, Taught and Schooled by Pain, once again I reiterate   is not merely a collection of experiences; it is a testament to the power of perseverance, a message to all celebrated champions and those still on their journey toward greatness.

To those fighting their own battles: stay in the ring. Don't let pain, losses, betrayals, rejections, or any hardship cause you to waver. Use every challenge as fuel, every setback as a steppingstone. The journey may be hard, but it is worth every moment. Champions are born not from comfort but from their unyielding commitment to stand strong and keep fighting.

AFTERWORD

As I pen these final words, I find myself reflecting on the journey of writing this book—a process that has been as transformative as the experiences that inspired it. Each chapter brought me back to moments in my own life when pain felt overwhelming, yet it also reminded me of the growth that emerged from those challenges. Writing about suffering, resilience, and healing has been a cathartic experience, allowing me to examine my own relationship with pain and the ways it has shaped my understanding of myself and my purpose. As I reflect on the journey shared within these pages, I am reminded of a profound truth: even in our most painful moments, God's presence remains steadfast. Throughout every trial, every loss, and every heartbreak, I have witnessed His unfailing assurance. Pain may be an isolating experience, but God's promise is that we are never truly alone.

In the hardest moments, when strength falters and hope feel distant, His presence becomes a source of comfort and resilience. It is this assurance—God's promise to walk with us, no matter the intensity of our struggles—that sustains us through pain and transforms it into growth.

He is not merely present as an observer but as a compassionate guide, working within us to bring meaning from even the deepest suffering.

'Taught and Schooled by Pain' reflects this truth. It is a story of God's power to turn adversity into strength and sorrow into purpose.

As you turn the last page, I hope you carry with you a renewed awareness of God's presence in your own journey. Trust that, no matter how heavy your burdens may feel, His love and guidance are unwavering, shaping each of us into something greater through every season of pain.

Throughout this process, I have come to appreciate the interconnectedness of our stories. In sharing the experiences of others alongside my own, I realized that pain is not a solitary journey; it is a collective experience that binds us together. Each narrative I explored was a reminder that, while our struggles may differ, the lessons we learn through them often resonate on a universal level. This realization has deepened my empathy for those around me and reinforced my belief in the power of vulnerability and connection.

In my own life, I continue to grow through the challenges I face. Each new hardship offers an opportunity to reflect, learn, and adapt. I have learned to embrace my emotions and acknowledge the discomfort that accompanies growth. I strive to see my struggles not as burdens but as teachers, guiding me toward a greater understanding of myself and my purpose.

The journey of healing is ongoing, and I am committed to nurturing resilience and compassion within myself and extending that kindness to others.

As readers, I hope you carry forward the lessons shared within these pages. May you find strength in your own struggles and view them as steppingstones toward a more profound sense of purpose. Remember that healing is not a destination, but a continuous journey filled with opportunities for growth, connection, and transformation.

Thank you for joining me on this exploration of pain and resilience. Together, let us embrace the complexities of our experiences and use them as fuel for a more compassionate and meaningful existence. May your path forward be illuminated by the strength you cultivate through every challenge, and may you continue to grow into the person you are meant to be.

APPENDICES

The journey through pain and the pursuit of healing and growth can be supported by a variety of resources and practical exercises. In this section, I have compiled additional readings, exercises for reflection, and resources to aid you in your personal journey.

FURTHER READINGS

1. **'The Body Keeps the Score' by Bessel van der Kolk**

   An exploration of how trauma affects both the body and mind, offering insights into healing through various therapeutic practices.

2. **'Rising Strong' by Brené Brown**

   A powerful look at how vulnerability can lead to resilience and strength, emphasizing the importance of embracing our stories.

3. **'Man's Search for Meaning' by Viktor E. Frankl**

   A profound reflection on finding purpose through suffering, based on Frankl's experiences in Nazi concentration camps.

4. **The Book of Job in the Bible** is one of the most profound texts addressing pain, suffering, and ultimately, triumph. Job's story is a testament to enduring faith amid unimaginable adversity. Stripped of his wealth, health, and family, Job faces a level of suffering that seems insurmountable. Yet, through his anguish, he clings to his faith and integrity, questioning yet never abandoning his relationship with God.

    In the end, Job's story is one of restoration and resilience. Though he confronts doubt, frustration, and confusion, Job's perseverance through suffering leads him to a deeper understanding of God's wisdom and sovereignty. His journey illustrates that while pain is part of life, it can ultimately lead to growth and a strengthened faith.

    For anyone navigating trials, Job offers hope and a reminder that pain does not have the final word. Instead, it can refine, transform, and deepen one's connection with God, underscoring the truth that His presence remains constant, even in our darkest hours.

APPENDIX B: PRACTICAL EXERCISES FOR REFLECTION

a. Journaling Prompts

1. Reflect on a painful experience and the lessons you learned from it. Which strengths did you uncover?
2. Write about a time when you supported someone else through their struggles. How did this experience impact you?
3. List three ways you can transform a current challenge into an opportunity for growth.

b. **Gratitude Practice**

Each day, write down three things you are grateful for, even if they are small. This practice helps shift your focus from pain to positivity.

c. **Mindfulness Meditation**

Set aside 10-15 minutes each day to sit in stillness. Focus on your breath and allow yourself to acknowledge any feelings or thoughts without judgment.

d. **Creating a Vision Board**

Gather images, quotes, and words that inspire you. Create a vision board that represents your goals for healing and growth. Display it in a place where you will see it daily.

e. **Acts of Kindness**

Choose one act of kindness each week to perform for someone else. Reflect on how this act impacts both you and the recipient.

APPENDIX C: ADDITIONAL RESOURCES

1. **Support Groups**
a. Explore local or online support groups related to your specific challenges, whether it be grief, addiction, trauma, or mental health.
2. **Therapy and Biblical Counselling**
a. Consider reaching out to a mental health professional for individual or group therapy to support your healing journey.
3. **Workshops and Retreats**
a. Look for my and others workshops or retreats focused on personal growth, resilience, and healing. These spaces often provide valuable tools and community support.
b. I do these workshop and retreats in different countries and cities, reach out to me, and get to know of my next workshop dates.

4. Podcasts

a. Tune in to my podcast and hear others share their stories of triumph and mine too around life's experiences.

b. Listen to podcasts that explore themes of pain, healing, and growth, such as 'Unlocking Us' by Brené Brown or 'Therapy Chat' for insights on trauma and healing.

FINAL THOUGHTS

Remember that, these appendices are intended to serve as tools to further support your journey beyond pain. Whether through readings, reflections, or resources, I hope you find inspiration and guidance as you navigate your unique path toward healing and growth. Remember, you are not alone in your struggles, and every step you take toward understanding and embracing your experiences is a step toward a brighter, more resilient future.

ABOUT THE AUTHOR

Dr. Herbert Mandla Mtowo

Dr. Herbert Mandla Mtowo is a passionate advocate for mental health and resilience, drawing from a diverse background in psychology, counselling, and personal development. Born and raised in a family of nine (9)), Dr. Mtowo's early experiences life`s experiences, death of his mother in his growing stages of his life, death of his brothers, death of his dad, relationship problems and his journey on difficult health issues, his experiences in travels is in Africa and working with different people from cultural backgrounds have shaped his understanding of the transformative power of pain and adversity. He pursued his education in psychology at Jacksonville Seminary, where he deepened his interest in the complexities of human emotions and the healing journey.

With over 20 years of experience working with less privileged communities, children and all, across Africa and some Asian countries, lecturing at Universities in Africa, in the mental health field, Psychology, and other commitments to community services, Dr. Mtowo has worked in various settings, including hospitals, community organizations, and private practice. His coaching and counselling work has focused on helping individuals navigate trauma, grief, and the challenges of everyday life. He believes that by confronting and embracing our pain, we can unlock profound personal growth and resilience.

Dr. Mtowo's motivations for writing *Taught and Schooled by Pain* stem from his desire to inspire others to view their struggles as opportunities for transformation. He understands that pain is an universal experience that can often feel isolated.

Through this book, he aims to foster connection, empathy, and hope, encouraging readers to see their own stories reflected in the experiences of his and others.

In addition to his work as a mental health professional, Dr. Mtowo is a sought-after speaker and workshop facilitator, sharing his insights on resilience, self-compassion, and the healing power of vulnerability. He continues to engage with communities through outreach programs, workshops facilitation and public speaking, aiming to break the stigma surrounding mental health and promote the importance of emotional well-being.

Dr. Mtowo believes in lifelong learning and remains committed to his own journey of growth, drawing inspiration from the stories of those he encounters along the way. Through his writing and advocacy, Dr. Mtowo hopes to empower individuals to embrace their pain, cultivate resilience, and ultimately transform their struggles into sources of strength and purpose. Dr Mtowo is a strong believer in God`s word as a manual to guide and help all in life`s challenges and grow through them.

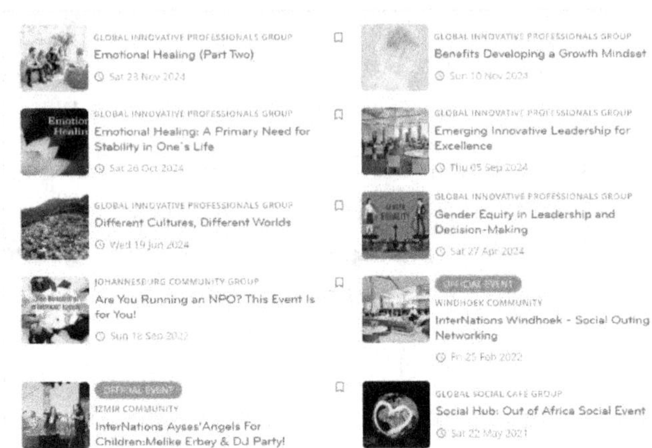

Some conferences by Dr Herbert Mandla Mtowo on an InterNations platform

References/Bibliography

i.   Brown, Brené. The Gifts of Imperfection: Let Go of Who You Think You're Supposed to Be and Embrace Who You Are. Hazelden Publishing, 2010.

ii.   Brown, Brené. Rising Strong: The Reckoning. The Rumble. The Revolution. Spiegel & Grau, 2015.

iii.   Kolk, Bessel van der. The Body Keeps the Score: Brain, Mind, and Body in the Healing of Trauma. Viking, 2014.

iv.   Goleman, Daniel. Emotional Intelligence: Why It Can Matter More Than IQ. Bantam Books, 1995.

v.   Seligman, Martin E.P. Flourish: A Visionary New Understanding of Happiness and Well-Being. Atria Books, 2011.

vi.   Nussbaum, Martha C. Upheavals of Thought: The Intelligence of Emotions. Cambridge University Press, 2001.

vii.   van der Kolk, Bessel A. "Trauma and Memory." Journal of Traumatic Stress, vol. 9, no. 3, 1996, pp. 515-520.

viii.   Gilbert, Paul. The Compassionate Mind: A New Approach to Life's Challenges. Constable, 2009.

ix.   The bible is full of life's painful experience turned into life's memorable victories.

We are taking action to protect nature.
This book contains only the necessary blank pages,
printed in black and white, and the book is only printed
when the reader orders it.
Thousands of trees are saved every year.